HOW TO SOLVE A MURDER

MICHAEL KURLAND

MACMILLAN • USA

MACMILLAN
A Simon & Schuster Macmillan Company
1633 Broadway
New York, NY 10019

MACMILLAN is a registered trademark of Macmillan, Inc.

Library of Congress Cataloging-in-Publication Data
Kurland, Michael.
  How to solve a murder: the forensic handbook/Michael Kurland.
    p.   cm.
  ISBN 0-02-860410-5
  1. Homicide investigation—United States—Handbooks, manuals, etc.
  2. Criminal investigation—United States—Handbooks, manuals, etc.
  3. Forensic sciences—United States—Handbooks, manuals, etc.
  I. Title.
HV8079.H6K87   1995   94-44327
363.2'59523'0973—dc20   CIP

10 9 8 7 6 5

Printed in the United States of America

ACKNOWLEDGMENTS

For his kind assistance in the preparation of this book I would like to thank Dr. Lawrence Kobilinsky of the John Jay College of Criminal Justice.

I thank the Research Unit of the Federal Bureau of Investigation Office of Public and Congressional Affairs.

Richard Schwoebel of Sandia Laboratories has also kindly given me his assistance.

My brother Frederick Kurland also gave to me unstintingly his time and advice. My sister-in-law Deirdre Kurland, a research biology technician, was good enough to correct my errors of fact, and occasionally of style, with patience and good humor.

Diana White Eagle, a fine artist, took time off from her painting to do—with her usual excellence—some of the technical drawing in this book.

For Frederick and Deirdre Kurland this book, and then some.

CONTENTS

HOW TO SOLVE A MURDER

INTRODUCTION

We all know how they catch criminals. We've read it in detective novels; we've seen it in the movies and on TV. "They," of course, are the police, or the G-men, or an intrepid private detective, or an international crime-fighting organization, or a hard-eyed private citizen pissed off at the ineptitude of law enforcement.

In fiction.

But the real criminals are caught by the real police, and given budget constraints and the complexity of our laws, they do a pretty good job of it. The successful detective combines an insight into the ways of criminals—born of years of experience—with the technical assistance of a team of forensic scientists who can squeeze an enormity of information from a few drops of clotted blood or a couple of hairs.

The public's perception of police work comes mainly from detective stories in books or on television—and a very strange and unnatural perception it is. The level of accuracy in these fictional accounts tends to be fairly low, the image of police procedure is often butchered, and the capabilities of scientific criminology are either ignored or grossly misrepresented. "Reality" cop shows concentrate on dramatic break-ins and the arrests of drug dealers, accompanied by a lot of cops shouting and suspects weeping. The private-eye shows follow the lead of private-eye literature in presenting cops as either antagonists or boobs—or both. Some police procedural books and shows try for a degree of accuracy

1

but often concentrate more on the detectives' job-related angst and relationship troubles than with the process of solving crimes.

The actual techniques of detective work and forensic analysis—two different yet allied arts with a common focus—are fascinating. Although long periods of tedious, routine work are a necessary part of the job, the results make all the effort worthwhile. After all, the hunting of humans has always been regarded by connoisseurs as the "greatest game." And when those being hunted are serial killers or sociopaths who consider murder an acceptable way of furthering their own careers, the satisfaction in taking one of these inhuman humans off the streets more than makes up for the boredom and routine.

In this book we will see how modern investigative techniques evolved and how such work is done in the United States today. By observing a fictional crime and following the detectives and criminalists as they work to solve it, we'll discover how the various forensic sciences have developed an arsenal of techniques for identifying and apprehending those who commit crimes.

Police departments are a comparatively new development in our society, dating back a scant hundred and fifty years. Detectives came in a few decades after that, and scientific criminal investigation emerged a couple of decades later. Before the establishment of organized police departments there existed a patchwork of constabulary, nightwatch, sheriffim, thief-takers, and other protectors of the peace. Insecure rulers maintained networks of spies and informants, but these men were interested in no crimes save plots against the king; in many cases they provoked such plots themselves, later "uncovering" them and thus proving their usefulness to their boss. The first police were also agents of the kings, existing to quell insurrections and riots, with the full power of the government behind them. Their function was more one of keeping down the "criminal classes" by any means necessary than seriously attempting to solve crimes.

POLICE POWER

Joseph Fouché, the Minister of Police in post-revolutionary France who set the course of both police and internal security functions in that country for the next two centuries, addressed the problem of police power in a circular sent to his subordinates dated November 21, 1799. The last paragraph reads:

> Never forget how dangerous it is to make arrests on mere suspicion; reflect that your actions, even when they are in error, will be a primary presumption against those whom you take before justice; and meditate in the quick of your conscience upon the history of so many innocent people who were sent by justice to the scaffold only because they were taken before justice in error.

Early detectives eschewed any attempt at what we would consider scientific criminology. They believed in criminal "types," and that a trained detective could pick out a criminal from a crowd of suspects by his appearance alone. To a certain extent this was true, but it was because society then was heavily stratified and lower-class felons were the only ones the police of the time were trained and equipped to catch. The "criminal type" theory is one reason why at the time of London's "Jack the Ripper" murders, speculation rose that Jack may have been a noble or even royal personage, or at the very least a member of the upper class. If he had been of the lower class, where the police concentrated their investigations, these speculators feel, he would have been caught.

Turn-of-the-century detectives would spend hours studying the "Rogues Galleries"—collections of photographs of known criminals, sometimes published as books to be distributed to all police jurisdictions. Police work was a rough-and-tumble exercise, where brawn was regarded as more important than brain and police officers with college degrees were suspect. But some early pioneers in police science, particularly Austria's Hanns Gross, France's Edmond Locard, and August Vollmer and O. W. Wilson of the United States, did much to professionalize police work and to encourage the application of scientific principles to investigative problems.

Many of the tools and techniques available to the scientific investigator today were not available as recently as ten years ago, and not even thought of twenty years ago. The tradition of continuous progress in forensic science began more than a century ago, yet it has been this century's cautiously innovative practitioners who have made possible the wonders of today.

DETECTION IN ANCIENT CHINA

Dutch Sinologist Robert van Gulik wrote a series of entertaining detective stories set in T'ang dynasty China. The hero of these tales, Judge Dee, is based on Ti Jen-chieh, a real magistrate who lived from 630 to 700 A.D.; Ti gained fame as an astute solver of complex crimes, rising in his career to serve at the highest levels of China's imperial government. Van Gulik based his tales on a body of seventeenth-century Chinese detective stories that featured Ti and other famous magistrates. These ancient stories show that the function of the criminal investigator was well understood in China long before it developed in the West.

Van Gulik's Judge Dee anticipated modern methods by a millennium: The procedure of the time called for the examination of witnesses, suspects, and physical evidence. When he didn't go forth himself (in disguise) to solve his cases, he used the services of investigators, and in suspected murder cases, he called upon medical experts to determine the cause of death. The culprit had to confess before he could be found guilty, but the magistrate could use torture to induce a confession. However, if the magistrate mistakenly tortured the wrong person, he himself would be subjected to the same tortures he had inflicted on the suspect (a prospect that no doubt had a wonderfully focussing effect on the investigation).

The fictional case we will follow in this book is an idealized and streamlined version of the forensic process. In showing how the forensic investigation develops evidence, we will leave out the hundreds of hours of investigation that are useful only in eliminating leads that do not pan out, a necessary but unexciting part of the investigator's routine. And we will be observing forensic technology at its most modern, which is not always the case in real life. Not all of today's leading-edge technology is to be found in any given police laboratory, and not all of what is available will be used in any given case, even when it perhaps should be—owing to the constraints of money, training, and influence.

Running a modern forensics laboratory and hiring competent personnel is expensive, and the budgets of most municipal and state governments today are stretched past the breaking point. The public perceives crime—especially violent crime—as on the increase and has reacted with anger and fear, but the response has not been what the forensic professional might wish: The legislatures have voted for millions of dollars to fund additional police officers and new prisons, and have passed laws increasing the severity of punishment for a wide variety of crimes. But new prisons and harsher laws attack the problem from the wrong end. There is general agreement among criminologists that it is the certainty of punishment, rather than its severity, that discourages criminals from committing crimes.

As for training, many employees of this country's forensic laboratories are inadequately, incompletely, or improperly trained. Technicians who are expert at taking and analyzing fingerprints may be called upon to type blood and other sera or to gather the evidence of blood splatters or toolmarks, often because no one else is available and because forensic technicians are assumed to be fungible. Ideally, technicians would be masters of a variety of tasks, but for that they must be trained for each individual specialty, and since some of the tasks are highly complex, this is often not the case. Thus within forensic laboratories there will still be a need for specialists; should expert services be needed, the pieces of physical evidence from a crime scene (known as exemplars) can be sent to the appropriate crime lab for examination.

When I cite the effect of "influence" on forensic examinations I'm speaking not so much of "improper" influence intended to physically prevent forensic scientists from doing their job, but rather the political influences that decide which cases are important and which are not. (A forensic technician is assigned to cases; he or she does not get to choose them.) When a high profile case surfaces—the death of a celebrity or a case involving a celebrity suspect, the eighth victim of a serial killer, or a crime on which a governor, mayor, or district attorney doesn't want to appear "soft"—then the full resources of the department are deployed. But the probable accidental death of John Doe may not even get a forensic team out to investigate it. And in localities where the forensic specialists are less than well trained, their tendency is to find what they expect to find and to dig no deeper. This is especially true of regular hospital pathologists, untrained in the criminal aspects of medicine, who are asked to perform forensic autopsies in jurisdictions that cannot afford the services of a full-time medical examiner. Medical pathologists are trained to identify disease, not crime. They look for pathogens, not poisons; heart attacks, not injections of insulin or the track of an icepick skillfully inserted in the ear.

On the reverse side of the coin there exists the terrible danger that an overzealous, poorly trained technician will read more into a crime scene's physical exemplars than the evidence warrants. In such situations the police and district attorney, predisposed to believe in the guilt of their suspect and conditioned to accept the word of their forensic technician as infallible truth, often will not look beyond the report, even when its weaknesses are evident.

This raises the even more frightening specter of the venial technician, interested more in pleasing the police or district attorney—and thus enhancing his own career—than in determining the truth and protecting the rights of the accused. In Texas a medical examiner recently was found to have fudged the results of hundreds of autopsies (the authorities are not sure how many) to get the results he thought the police wanted. His motives are not clear, but the result is that now, in any case where the examiner had supplied substantial medical evidence that lead to a conviction, the defendant has a strong case for appeal. There is also the definite possibility that some of those were actually wrongly convicted and are in fact innocent. In New York State at the present time there is an ongoing investigation of technicians in the State Police who may have forged the fingerprints of suspects to strengthen the cases against them.

Criminalists must always be aware that they owe their first duty to the truth; unbendable, unshakable, influenced only by the physical evidence they have collected and the information that their instruments and their knowledge have been able to draw from that evidence. They must be able to explain their conclusions to the authorities and in court in such a way that the listeners understand the parameters of the truths they are hearing. They must, for example, realize and convey the fact that a high probability is not an absolute. That, as someone once put it, if a suspect is "one in a million," there are a dozen others just like him within a five-mile radius of Times Square.

Former Connecticut state's attorney Homer S. Cummings is an example of the sort of independent, unprejudiced thinking for which an investigator should strive. In 1924, Cummings, a popular Democrat being groomed to run for governor in an upcoming election, was assigned to prosecute Harold Israel, a twenty-three-year-old drifter from Pennsylvania, for the murder of Fr. Hubert Dahme, pastor of Saint Joseph's Episcopal Church in Bridgeport. On February 4 of that year, Father Dahme had been gunned down on the street in front of his church.

The evidence seemed overwhelming: The police had wrung a confession from Israel, he was in possession of a handgun of the caliber that had killed Father Dahme, several eyewitnesses claimed to have seen Israel do the deed, and a ballistics expert tied the murder bullet to Israel's gun.

It was open-and-shut. Given the mood of the people—Father Dahme had been very popular in his community—the conviction would be celebrated, and Cummings would be a shoo-in to occupy the governor's mansion.

Cummings, in preparing his case, carefully checked the facts and discovered that they didn't add up. The eyewitnesses couldn't have seen what they claimed to have seen from where they were standing. Six new ballistics experts, each working separately, unanimously concluded that the murder bullet did not come from Israel's gun. And to top it off, Cummings discovered that Israel's gun had a defective firing pin and would not fire when pointed downward at the angle from which the murder weapon must have been fired.

Cummings demonstrated this in court, dramatically pointing the loaded gun at the floor and clicking the trigger. The judge directed that Israel be released, and Cummings personally escorted the young man to the train station, where he was soon bound for Pennsylvania.

The result was not popular; the citizens of Connecticut wanted someone to swing for Father Dahme's murder. Cummings was not elected governor. Instead he became Franklin D. Roosevelt's attorney general. And in 1947, twenty-three years after the Israel case, a movie was made of the story: *Boomerang* starred Dana Andrews and was directed by Elia Kazan.

The three facets of proving the guilt of a suspect are said to be motive, means, and opportunity. The greater degree of each that can be shown, the greater the probability of apprehending and convicting the guilty person. The criminalist can help to establish the means and opportunity, and occasionally can even say something useful about the motive.

Let us, in a highly artificial but possibly revealing manner, grade these three aspects in a mythical crime:

> *Who killed Cock Robin?*
> *"I," said the Sparrow.*
> *"With my bow and arrow,*
> *"I killed Cock Robin."*

Let us, not taking the Sparrow's confession for granted, examine the little bird's motive, means, and opportunity, rating each on a scale of zero to five:

Motive:

0 It cannot be shown that the Sparrow had ever met Cock Robin or had any reason to have ill feelings about him.

1 The Sparrow and Cock Robin were business rivals, but being a bird is not a highly competitive business.

2 The Sparrow and Cock Robin had been heard to have words over a choice nesting site.

3 The Sparrow thought that Cock Robin had taken Sparrow's chick away from him, and was believed to be brooding about it.

4 The Sparrow believed that Cock Robin had murdered Sparrow's parents, and had told friends that he was just waiting for a chance to get his talons on said Cock Robin.

5 The Sparrow was just beaten up by Cock Robin, and had been seen picking up his bow and arrow, pursuing his assailant, and muttering, "That bird won't live to see another sunrise!"

Means:

0 The Sparrow, due to an old injury, was unable to pull back a bowstring.

1 The Sparrow was not known to own a bow and arrow, but had taken archery at Bird U.

2 The Sparrow was an ardent archer and owned quite a selection of little bows and arrows.

3 The arrow found in poor Cock Robin's body was similar to those used by the Sparrow.

4 The Sparrow was seen to have a bow with him at lunch, which resembled one found at the murder scene. He claimed it had been stolen from him.

5 The arrow protruding from Cock Robin's red breast had the Sparrow's wingprints all over it. DNA fingerprinting of a feather found at the scene matched the Sparrow's.

Opportunity:

0 The Sparrow was at the White House, having lunch with the President at the time of the murder.

1 The Sparrow states he had been playing poker with three close buddies, who back up his story.

2 The Sparrow claims to have been at the opera (*Lohengrin*) and even has the ticket stub, but saw nobody he knew there who could corroborate his story.

3 The Sparrow was in the area of the murder, but nobody can place him at the scene.

4 The Sparrow was seen leaving the scene but claims Cock Robin was dead when he arrived.

5 The Sparrow, bow in wing, was found standing over the body of the victim as Cock Robin breathed his last.

If the three numbers derived from the Motive, Means, and Opportunity lists total zero, you had better start looking for another suspect. If they total fifteen, you can tell the judge it would be unwise to offer bail before the trial (in those states that allow bail in a murder case). A prosecutor would like to have a total of ten or higher on our hypothetical scale before going to trial.

A statement often heard in criminal law is that guilt is something determined by a jury. Since we do not yet possess the ability to peer into the mind of another, it is possible to establish the guilt of a defendant to a moral certainty, but not as an absolute fact. Should you ever find yourself saying, "He did this, or I'm a monkey's uncle," remember that there is a small but finite chance that your nephew *is* a monkey. Eyewitnesses can be, and often are, mistaken; circumstantial evidence, on the whole more reliable, can be misinterpreted; and the rush to judgment can sometimes pass right by the truth. A 1987 report by the *Stanford Law Review* asserts that from 1900 to 1985 at least twenty-seven of those people executed in the United States were innocent of the crimes for which they were convicted, and an article by John Horgan in the July 1990 *Scientific American* states that at least twenty-seven people sentenced to death in the past eighteen years alone have later been found innocent by a higher court.

It seems to be human nature to reduce problems as quickly as possible to yes-or-no, right-or-wrong answers. Sometimes the reduction happens so quickly that our minds don't even see the middle ground passing us by.

THE CRIME

> *If once a man indulges himself in murder, very soon he comes to think little of robbing; and from robbing he comes next to drinking and Sabbath-breaking, and from that to incivility and procrastination.*
>
> —THOMAS DE QUINCEY,
> *MURDER CONSIDERED AS ONE OF THE FINE ARTS*

Let us now arrange for a crime being committed; a fictional crime, a mythical murder, which we shall tailor to our needs. We will observe our murderer as he goes about his nefarious deed. He will be an average murderer; not especially bright, not overly dense, yet highly motivated to get away with his crime. The murderers of fiction, who compound their crimes with a series of acts designed to fool the police, who create perfect locked-room mysteries that only the fictional sleuth can solve, do not exist in real life. A real murderer is not interested in fooling the detectives; he is interested in not getting caught. The few real-life killers who have devised complex schemes designed to misdirect or baffle the authorities are usually sociopathic personalities who are so convinced of their own superiority that they overlook simple details that lead the investigators right to them. One thinks of Leopold and Loeb, who dropped a pair of glasses while disposing of the body of poor Bobby Franks; or of Ruth Snyder, who claimed her husband had been killed by burglars, but who hid her supposedly stolen jewelry under her mattress, where the police found it.

Once our mythical murder has been committed and the criminal has escaped, we will watch the criminalists at work, and oversee their attempt to unravel the puzzle. Thus we can focus on those details that will best show the process.

And so:

The Location: Gotham City, a medium-sized city in the eastern United States, with a mixed ethnic population of close to two million (including the suburbs) fairly well-behaved citizens. The police force is adequate for a city of this size, although Police Commissioner Gordon feels that he could put fifty more police officers to good use if the city council could find the money. Gotham's crime lab, a modern, up-to-date facility, is staffed with a mix of sworn officers and civilian technicians, all of whom are proficient at their jobs. For some of the more specialized or complex procedures, such as DNA profiling, the lab sends its exemplars to the FBI lab in Washington, D.C., or to one of the certified private laboratories around the country.

The Victim: Prominent criminal attorney Godfrey Daniels, who is reputed to have been a silent partner to many of the criminals he has defended.

The Criminal: Philomar "The Yegg" Yancy, a stick-up artist and small-time hoodlum who had been a client of Counselor Daniels for many years.

The Motive: Fear and greed.

The Crime: Murder.

THE EVENT

It would be wrong to say that Yancy planned to commit murder; rather, let us say he was not averse to the deed if it proved necessary. A tall, thin man with a prominent nose and the peculiar habit of darting his head about like a pigeon on the lookout for hawks, Yancy would not have been insulted if you called him a criminal. He got his start at the age of seven, when, after taking a chocolate bar from the candy counter at Megram's, it occurred to him that if he put it in his pocket when no one was looking, he wouldn't have to pay for it. It was downhill from there.

Around seven o'clock on a chilly Saturday evening in October, Yancy parked his nondescript green sedan in the service alley behind a row of expensive houses in the Richwood section of Gotham City. The third house from the corner, a two-story pseudo-Tudor mansionette, was the home of attorney Godfrey Daniels. Its small backyard was fenced in and apparently saw little use; backyards were unnecessary appendages to the houses of people who were all front. A garage, used for storage and for the Daniels' four-wheel drive "country car," faced the service alley. Husband and wife parked their luxury sedans in their front driveway to reassure the neighbors.

Daniels was not only Yancy's lawyer but also had a profitable sideline fencing the goods stolen by Yancy and other clients (only the most valuable items, of course: jewelry, stamp and coin collections, *objets d'art*, etcetera). It was an avocation his wife knew nothing about. Yancy was visiting Daniels this evening to discuss some new acquisitions, and though his appointment was for eight o'clock, he wanted the extra hour to reconnoiter. Yancy needed to assure himself he wasn't being set-up by the criminous criminal lawyer and to secure his means of retreat in case Yancy was forced to do what he firmly told himself he had no intention of doing.

In one of his more successful midnight forays a week earlier, Yancy had acquired several pieces of jewelry whose retail value was in excess of half a million dollars. Daniels, in an artfully indirect telephone conversation, had offered Yancy $10,000 for the pieces. Yancy had suggested ten times that. Daniels had told Yancy to come over at eight o'clock, and something could be worked out. Yancy, having negotiated with Daniels before, thought he could improve the results if he had a gun. After all, Daniels couldn't very well complain that he was being robbed.

There is a mindset often found in career criminals that enables them to blame everyone else for their own misfortunes and predations. "I didn't want to kill him, it's his own fault for resisting" or "If he didn't want me to mug him, he shouldn't have walked down the street." Yancy, whose mind moved firmly along this track, was convinced Daniels was trying to cheat him (which might well have been so) and therefore anything that happened to Daniels was the crooked lawyer's own fault.

Or so reasoned Mr. Yancy.

Yancy removed the .32-caliber Walther automatic from his glove compartment, pulled back the slide to chamber a round, and stuck the gun in his belt. Just for protection and, if necessary, persuasion, he reminded himself firmly—not for use. Stepping out of his car, he carefully skirted the mud puddles left from the day's earlier rain and walked to the end of the alley. The rears of the buildings were devoid of activity; nobody to remark on his comings or goings. The few lighted windows that faced the rear were closed against the chill October air, and nobody seemed likely to peer out in the faint hope that there would be anything to see.

Yancy left the alley, walking around the corner and up the street to the Daniels's house. He cased the house carefully without stopping, so as not to draw attention to himself. The only car in Daniels's driveway was the attorney's large black Mercedes Benz,which meant the wife wasn't home. That was good.

Yancy went back to his car and sat for the rest of the hour, smoking and brooding, talking himself into what he kept telling himself he wasn't planning to do. At about ten to eight he tossed his last cigarette butt out the window, left the car again, and went around to the Daniels's front door.

Daniels, a chunky, well-groomed man of average height who radiated arrogance and confidence if not charm, answered the door promptly. The lawyer took Yancy into the large ground-floor room to the right of the entrance hall which served as his study; if he noticed that Yancy was nervous and tense he said nothing. It was not unusual for those who visited him—either in his capacity as a criminal lawyer or in one of the other roles his criminal practice had led him into—to be both tense and nervous.

"Well, you've been an active little boy, haven't you?" Daniels asked, smiling pleasantly. Calling Yancy a little boy was not a way to win his confidence or admiration, but this was of small concern to the lawyer.

Yancy suppressed his ire and glanced nervously around. "Are we alone?"

"You hardly suppose I'd want witnesses, do you?" Daniels opened a cabinet and poured two glasses of scotch, dumped a couple of ice cubes from an ice bucket into the glasses, and passed one of the drinks to Yancy.

"I have no idea what you want—besides the swag," Yancy said.

Daniels settled himself in behind his desk and waved Yancy to a red leather chair across from him. "Swag!" he said. "Thieves' cant for stolen goods. Dates from the twenties, I believe. I've never actually heard anyone say 'swag' before."

"I read it in a book," Yancy said. He pulled a leather sack from his pocket, unzipped it, and dumped the contents on the desk. "Well?"

Daniels turned on his desk light and picked up the pieces one at a time—a necklace sparkling with walnut-sized diamonds and emeralds; a bracelet that seemed to gather the light to itself and throw it forth again, magnified many times over; a pair of matching earrings; and some lesser pieces, each worth awed attention in less-glamorous company. "Hmm," he said, taking a jeweler's loupe from his pocket and staring in evident fascination at the necklace.

"They're worth over half a million," Yancy said. "The television news said so. I want a hundred thousand. It's only fair."

Daniels put down the loupe. "They always exaggerate on the news, makes for a better story. Close to half a million retail, maybe," he said. "Wholesale is half of that, if you're lucky. And they'll have to be broken up. The individual stones won't bring as much." He reached into the top drawer of his desk and pulled out a packet of bills. "Here," he said, tossing it across the desk. "Best I can do."

Yancy riffled the stack of bills. "Ten thousand," he said.

"A good night's work," Daniels commented, sweeping the jewelry on the desk toward him. "Take it."

"Not enough," Yancy said.

"It's all I'm going to give you. It's generous. You have to understand . . ."

"No," Yancy said, standing up abruptly, stuffing the money in his pocket, and pulling the automatic from another pocket. "*You* have to understand. I've been swindled by you too often. Either give me the whole hundred thousand or give me the stuff back."

Daniels put his hands flat on the desk and glared at Yancy. "If you think to frighten me, you're mistaken. Shooting me won't get you another dime."

"I'll just have to go elsewhere," Yancy said, gesturing with the gun. "Push the stones back over here!"

Whether Daniels was overcome by greed or just didn't believe Yancy would shoot will never be known. With one gesture he swept the gems into his desk drawer and pulled out his own gun.

Yancy fired first. The slug entered Daniels's chest above the heart, severing several important arteries. Daniels fired, his bullet nicking Yancy on the left arm and then burying itself in the far wall; Yancy reflexively dropped his gun and clutched at his wound. Daniels staggered around the desk, blood spurting from his chest, and attempted to raise his gun again. He grabbed for Yancy, who broke free with an almost superstitious panic and pushed him away. Daniels stumbled, brushing several things off the desk and upsetting a wastebasket, and then collapsed on his back. He was in shock. In a matter of seconds he would be dead.

Yancy stood for a moment unable to move. As his panic subsided he saw that Daniels had expired on the floor; there was no sign that the gunfire had attracted any attention. Holding his arm to staunch the flow from his minor but bloody wound, he peered closely at Daniels to make sure he was dead, and then stepped over the body and circled the desk. Yancy scooped the jewelry up and put it in his pocket. He did a quick search of the desk, picking up a few hundred dollars from one of the drawers and a pair of gold cufflinks from another.

Yancy then entered the bathroom adjoining the study, where he took off his jacket and rolled up his sleeve to look at the wound. Satisfied that it was little more than a scratch, he held some toilet paper over the wound until it stopped bleeding. Finding some bandages in the medicine cabinet, he ripped one open and plastered it over the wound. After carefully rolling his shirt sleeve back down, Yancy took a wad of toilet paper and went over everything he had touched in the bathroom and cleaned every place he could find where drops of blood had fallen. When he had finished and had flushed the wad of paper down the toilet, the bathroom looked reasonably neat. His jacket was too bloody to wear, so he went upstairs, located Daniels's bedroom, and took one of the man's sport jackets. The fit was poor, but Yancy wouldn't be wearing it long. While in the bedroom, he took a couple of minutes to explore the room, taking a few pieces of jewelry, an expensive watch, and some cash he found in the bureau drawers.

Returning to the study, Yancy took one of the small guest towels from the bathroom and wiped off everything he could remember touching or thought he might have touched. Almost as an afterthought he picked up his gun from the floor and stuffed it into the pocket of his newly acquired jacket. He wiped the glass Daniels had handed him, the front of the desk, and the doorknob. Then, rolling the bloody jacket and towel into a bundle and tucking it under his arm, Yancy made his way through the house to the back door and out into the yard. The door in the fence had a spring-latch lock that didn't need a key from the inside; Yancy went through and closed it behind him. He knew he shouldn't hurry—

he didn't want to draw attention to himself—but it took all his will-power not to break into a run back to his car.

He sat in the car for a few minutes to catch his breath and watch the street. No one came running out; no lights suddenly went on—or off—in any of the windows. It seemed that nobody had noted his coming or would note his leaving. Yancy started his car and slowly drove away from the Daniels home. He would get rid of the gun and the bloody clothing, he thought, and then there would be nothing to connect him with the murder of Godfrey Daniels.

He drove for about two miles, finally stopping in an alley in a business area to shove the gun deep into a Dumpster behind the Penguin Club, a popular restaurant. The clothing he took home to cut into small pieces and burn.

ONE

THE SPECIALISTS

Modern police science may be said to have three phases. The first phase embraces the identification of living and dead persons. The second embraces the field work carried out by specially trained detectives at the scene of the crime. The third embraces methods used in the police laboratory to examine and analyze clues and traces discovered in the course of the investigation.

— HARRY SÖDERMAN AND JOHN J. O'CONNELL,
MODERN CRIMINAL INVESTIGATION

Before we watch the Gotham City Police Department go about the process of investigating the murder of attorney Godfrey Daniels, let us take a brief overview of the specialties involved. There are many things that a properly equipped police laboratory staffed by well-trained technicians can contribute to the solution of crimes. If a scientific investigation is conducted at crime scene before anything present has been moved, touched, or trampled down, an amazing amount of data can be recovered for investigation and analysis. Much of it may prove to have little or no bearing on the crime, but two or three hairs found on the victim's body, fiber particles taken from the victim's clothing, a partial fingerprint lifted from the victim's skin, or DNA typing of blood or semen found on the scene may be what is needed to locate, identify, and convict the perpetrator.

Different jurisdictions handle their crimes in different ways. Due to lack of funds, imagination, or interest, some are not as modern as we would like. Others are as up to date as their judicial system will permit, developing every sort of clue that the court will allow.

The term *forensic* refers to that which is used by the courts. In oratory it describes a speech crafted to show one side of an argument or pleading. In criminology it has come to be the adjective prefix to the names of certain branches of science, to indicate the specialized use of that science to aid in solving crimes. The list of scientific specialties that have evolved to detect and apprehend criminals is large and surprisingly varied. It includes:

FINGERPRINT EXPERTS

Dactyloscopy, the scientific study of fingerprints, was first developed nearly a hundred years ago to identify convicts. When law enforcers realized that fingerprints are also left behind on all manner of surfaces, the use was extended to catching criminals as well. With some recent additions to the original bag of tricks, dactyloscopy is still an important weapon in the crimestopper's arsenal.

CRIME SCENE PHOTOGRAPHERS

A crime scene must be photographed from every angle to clearly show every detail, with emphasis on accurately recording the size and distance of objects. The crime scene photographer, whose work often involves the use of specialized cameras and film, may also be trained in fingerprint lifting and analysis, and may be called the Identification Officer or Identification Technician.

FORENSIC PATHOLOGISTS

Forensic pathologists, employed by the office of the medical examiner, determine the time and cause of death in cases of suspected homicide or suicide. The medical examiner's office is also often responsible for local public health issues such as investigating suspected cases of plague or other highly dangerous infectious diseases.

Other medical specialties that may aid in criminal investigation are:

FORENSIC PSYCHOLOGISTS AND PSYCHIATRISTS

Forensic psychologists or psychiatrists may be called on to evaluate a murder scene to suggest a possible psychological profile of the killer. The FBI has done much work in developing such profiles of serial killers and will often send one of its experts to assist the local police.

FORENSIC SEROLOGISTS

Forensic serology is the study of blood groups, blood, and other bodily fluids for identification purposes following a crime. Forensic serologists are also on the forefront of the new techniques of DNA fingerprinting, which offer the possibility of positive identification of an individual by any available body cells.

FORENSIC DENTISTS AND ODONTOLOGISTS

Forensic dentists or odontologists examine the teeth of corpses for identification purposes or make casts of human bite marks in foods—sometimes in people—to match the bite with the biter.

And outside the medical field, there are:

BALLISTICS EXPERTS

From the Roman *ballista*, a sort of heavy-duty slingshot, ballistics began as the study of the flight paths of projectiles. By extension, ballistics experts are now experts in the study of everything to do with firearms.

FORENSIC CHEMISTS

Forensic chemists specialize in analyzing such things as tiny chips of paint to determine the color and manufacturer, as well as determining the identity of minuscule amounts of drugs, dyes, and other chemicals and random unidentified particles.

FORENSIC GEOLOGISTS

Forensic geologists can determine such things as where the suspect or victim walked by examining soil samples taken from their shoes or feet.

FORENSIC ENTOMOLOGISTS

Forensic entomologists are specialists in the study of insects. In a murder investigation, these experts can determine how long a body has been dead by the degree of development of the maggots growing on it.

FORENSIC ANTHROPOLOGISTS

Forensic anthropologists can, from examining a pile of bones, determine not only whether or not they are human remains, but can also supply a surprising amount of detail about what the person looked like, and often how the person died.

FORENSIC ARTISTS

Forensic artists can draw a likeness of a person based solely on eyewitness descriptions, and can age a portrait to illustrate what a sixty-year-old subject would look like today based on a photograph taken at age thirty-five.

FORENSIC SCULPTORS

Forensic sculptors can reconstruct, usually in modelling clay, the appearance of a face from the structure of the skull, sometimes with startling accuracy.

FORENSIC LINGUISTS

Forensic linguists analyze the content of written or aural communication to identify who is speaking and indicate the speaker's intent, and can determine whether two communications are from the same person.

Since police procedures vary not only from state to state but from town to town (much as the FBI would like to standardize them) we will try to make the procedures used by our fictitious Gotham City Police Force and its criminalists as average as possible. The crime investigation itself will be earnestly up-to-date but will use no techniques not in use in the crime labs of major police forces around the country.

Gotham City's crime lab is staffed by professional criminalists—trained forensic scientists with graduate-level degrees in forensic science—who are knowledgeable in several disciplines. To start with, they will be expert at crime scene investigation and analysis, including fingerprinting, latent-fingerprint lifting, crime scene photography, and the taking and preserving of exemplars (bits of potential evidence) such as blood, saliva, or semen stains; hair and fabric samples; and mud, dust, pollen, and other meaningful minutia.

Back in the lab these experts will be able to handle any forensic investigation that doesn't require highly technical knowledge and equipment—as DNA fingerprinting does at the present time—or a breadth of institutional knowledge such as is found at the FBI's crime laboratory. Many exemplars could well be sent to the FBI, which has collections of standards against which to test paint, typewriting samples, watermarks, shoe sole and heel designs, tire tread designs, and many other such items identifiable by type.

But it would not do to forget that for all of the assistance of the criminalists in making a case, the burden of finding, assembling, and interpreting the evidence remains in the hands of the detectives. Their training and expertise is as important as that of the forensic specialists.

Now let us follow the Gotham City police force and crime lab as they investigate the murder of attorney Godfrey Daniels.

THE INVESTIGATION

> *There has been murder done, and the murderer was a man. He was more than six feet high, was in the prime of life, had small feet for his height, wore coarse, square-toed boots, and smoked a Trichinopoly cigar.*
>
> —ARTHUR CONAN DOYLE,
> *A STUDY IN SCARLET*

Murder is properly regarded as the most serious of crimes. Only kidnapping warrants the devotion of more police resources. And the reason kidnapping has as high a priority is the knowledge that in such a case, rapid and intelligent police work—with a little luck—might prevent a murder.

We will follow the progress of the murder investigation in Gotham City, with digressions along the way to describe which aspects of it were done elsewhere, or to add other facts of interest. The Godfrey Daniels investigation began, as you might expect, when someone called the police to report a murder.

THE CALL

It was 9:32 on a chilly Saturday evening in October when the call came in to Gotham City's 911 emergency number. A distraught voice told the operator, "My husband has been killed."

The emergency operator immediately dispatched a police patrol car in the area to the scene of the crime, while attempting to calm down the speaker and obtain some relevant facts. This information was relayed to the uniformed police officers in the patrol car as they approached the scene, informing them of the situation they would be facing and including pertinent information such as whether the killer was believed to be on the premises.

The patrol car (called a *unit* in police parlance) was dispatched to the home of Godfrey Daniels in the Richwood section of Gotham City, an area populated by some of Gotham City's wealthier citizens. Seven minutes after the call came in the unit arrived at the scene. The two officers quickly ascertained that there was indeed the corpse of a middle-aged man lying on the floor in the study to the right of the front door. There were signs of a struggle, and the man appeared to have been shot. A hysterical woman identified herself as Mrs. Cecilia Daniels and the corpse as that of her husband, Godfrey, a prominent local attorney.

THE FIRST OFFICERS

The two uniformed patrol persons now became, technically, the "first officers" at the crime scene. As such they had a variety of very important—and sometimes mutually contradictory—tasks to perform. First they had to make sure that the victim was indeed dead. If there was any chance that he wasn't, the officers would have called for an emergency ambulance. As there appeared to be no question regarding the man's current state, the men called for the homicide squad, who in turn called for the medical examiner—the victim wasn't *really* dead until the medical examiner said so.

Next the officers had to make sure the suspect was not on the premises or loitering in the vicinity. If a suspect were present, it would have been their happy task to apprehend him or her.

The men had to accomplish these two tasks without in any way disturbing the crime scene or allowing anyone else to disturb it. Frequently it is difficult to tell whether a person is dead without disturbing the body or its surroundings. Worse, there will often be a horde of people intent on tramping through the crime scene, including the residents of the building where the crime was committed, their friends and neighbors, reporters and television crews, and other police officers. All must be kept away so that the homicide detectives and the crime lab officers can have as pristine a scene as possible to investigate.

The solution to many a famous or important crime has been hampered by a failure to keep the scene of the crime sacrosanct. Neighbors roaming through the Borden house destroyed or carried off as souvenirs much potential evidence that might have established whether Lizzie Borden did or did not wield the ax used to murder her father and stepmother. Platoons of New Jersey state and local police swarmed around the Lindbergh house after the Lindbergh baby was kidnapped, making it impossible to determine whether the footprints in the flower bed were those of the kidnapper or one of the state troopers. And one crucial piece of evidence brought out at the trial of Bruno Richard Hauptmann, the Lindbergh baby's accused kidnapper, was a telephone number written in pencil on a doorjamb in his house; it was later found to have been put there by a reporter in an attempt to enhance a story, but by then Hauptmann had been executed.

When the Gotham City officers arrived at the Daniels house, they found Mrs. Daniels trying to clean the study in which her husband's body was lying. This is a surprisingly frequent response, and was not regarded as a sign of guilt but as a normal reaction to the stress of the moment. Mrs. Daniels just didn't want the detectives to enter a messy house. The officers kindly but firmly dissuaded her from continuing her house cleaning until after the investigators had finished their poking, prodding, peering, and dusting for fingerprints—by which time her urge would probably have passed.

The first officers must be aware of and prevent many normal actions that become inappropriate at a crime scene. No one should use the toilet, run water, wash or wipe their hands, use the telephone, drink out of glasses or cups, or handle objects or touch furniture at the scene. Any of these things could turn out to provide evidence.

And the officers must be aware of their own actions. When Marilyn Sheppard was murdered in her bedroom in a Cleveland suburb in 1957 (a case that will be examined in detail in a later chapter), her husband, Dr. Samuel Sheppard, was the prime suspect. One of the first people on the scene noticed the butt of a non-filtered cigarette floating in the toilet bowl of the upstairs bathroom. Dr. Sam was not a smoker; Marilyn seldom smoked, and then only filtered brands. But when an investigator went to collect the butt for evidence, it was discovered that one of the police officers on the scene had flushed it down the toilet.

The first officers must keep notes of everything, including all relevant times: the time they were called, the time they arrived, the time the crime was committed (if that can be established), and the times various people arrive on or leave the scene. They should also note the state or condition of anything that could change or be changed before the homicide detectives arrive: Are the lights on or off? Are the windows open or closed? Are the blinds up or down? Can the officers smell cigarette smoke? Perfume? Gunpowder? Are there any used cups, glasses, or dishes in evidence? Are there any visible footprints or fingerprints?

Unless the homicide detectives arrive almost immediately, the first officers also conduct the preliminary interviews. They should try to keep the witnesses apart so they don't have a chance to discuss their recollections with each other, especially if any of them are suspected of involvement in the crime. If the witnesses cannot be separated physically, they should be instructed not to discuss the facts with each other. It is very important to get what facts are available while they are fresh in the minds of the witnesses. A psychological phenomenon causes people to reconstruct events in their own minds according to what they hear from others, therefore witnesses should be questioned separately and their stories taken down in as much detail as possible before they have a chance to discuss the events with others.

The first officers have a difficult and thankless job. The importance of what they do is not recognized unless they screw up, in which case they will hear about it endlessly from the detectives and from their sergeant.

THE HOMICIDE DETECTIVES

The next to arrive at the Daniels home were a pair of detectives from the homicide squad. They would stay with the case from that moment until the successful prosecution of the perpetrator or until their retirement from the force—the book on a murder case is never closed until the case is solved. Because Gotham City has only one homicide division, located in the police headquarters building, detectives often arrive at the crime scene a half an hour to an hour after the first officers.

In many areas the name of the homicide squad has been changed to the Major Crimes Unit (or Squad) in recognition of the fact that homicide officers regularly investigate other crimes, including kidnapping, rape, assault with intent to kill, and any assaults with weapons.

THE FIRST DETECTIVE

In 1828 Eugéne François Vidocq, head of the French police service, wrote his memoirs, giving the public its first view of the life of a police officer. Vidocq, who spent the first half of his life as a criminal and therefore understood them very well, made most of his arrests by wandering in disguise among the criminal classes and listening to their conversations. But his knowledge of criminal methods enabled him to anticipate and thus foil many illegal enterprises. As he put it:

> Each day increased the number of my discoveries. Of the many who were committed to prison, there were none who did not owe their arrest to me, and yet not one of them for a moment suspected my share in the business. I managed so well, that neither within nor without its walls, had the slightest suspicion transpired. The thieves of my acquaintance looked upon me as their best friend and true comrade; the others esteemed themselves happy to have an opportunity of initiating me in their secrets, whether from the pleasure of conversing with me, or in the hope of benefiting by my counsels.

When the homicide officers arrived they first had to ascertain that a crime had been committed. Mr. Daniels was lying dead on his study floor, but it had yet to be determined how he got that way. The evidence of the first officers and any witnesses on the scene gave strong indications, but homicide detectives are taught to rely on their own intelligence guided by experience. Many cases that appear to be accidental death or suicide have turned out to be homicide, and not a few cases of apparent homicide have turned out to be accidental death.

If the homicide detectives decide that the death is "suspicious," either homicide or suicide, then the medical examiner's office is notified and the police forensic unit is summoned. This unit goes by different names in different jurisdictions—the Major Crime Scene Unit, the Identification Section, the Technical Squad or the Forensic Investigations Unit.

In areas where there is no forensic unit, the homicide detectives themselves must act as crime scene investigators, aided by whatever specialized personnel the department does have, such as ballistics experts or fingerprint specialists.

In any case the homicide detectives must be familiar enough with the procedures to understand the methods and the conclusions drawn from them, since they will be using the information both to apprehend the guilty party and to shape the prosecutor's case before it goes to trial.

One important difference between homicide investigations and those of other major crimes is that the notes and reports on a homicide must be more complete, more detailed, and more clearly written. Because a homicide case is never closed until it is solved, a new investigator must be able to reconstruct the case from the notes and reports perhaps a decade or two after the event.

In pursuing the case of the defunct Mr. Daniels, we will follow each of the specialists in turn, to see how they operate and what can be learned from their area of expertise. The people in charge of the case are the homicide detectives, and all information developed will be supplied to them for their consideration and action.

The homicide detectives themselves have an established set of priorities to follow. Each team will more or less do things their own way depending on local habits and customs, their own training, and the way they evaluate each case. Usually the first thing they will do, after making sure that the crime scene is secure, is question the witnesses.

Unless the homicide team was able to respond very quickly, the first officers will have taken preliminary statements and cautioned the witnesses not to discuss the events with one another. The detectives will then question the witnesses in depth, attempting to establish as much information about the events as possible.

An important difference separates witnesses from suspects. Witnesses may be questioned in detail and at length to the extent that they are willing and able to assist the detective. Suspects can only be questioned after they are advised of their Miranda rights.

THE MIRANDA RULE

A person suspected of a crime cannot be questioned by the police until he or she is advised of the right to keep silent and to have a lawyer present at any interrogation. If the suspect is not so informed, whatever is said cannot be used against him or her in court, and no information derived from the answers can be used. Called the Miranda Rule, this procedure is based on the right against self-incrimination assured by the Fifth Amendment.

The usual form of warning, often printed on a card and read to the suspect, goes something like:

> You have the right to remain silent. If you give up this right, what you say may be taken down and used in evidence against you in a court of law. You have the right to have an attorney present during questioning. If you cannot afford an attorney one will be provided for you. Do you understand these rights?

The rule comes from the case of *Miranda* v. *Arizona*, which was decided by the Supreme Court on June 13, 1966. In 1963 Ernesto Miranda was tried in an Arizona court for kidnapping and rape. He had previously been identified by the victim and, following a two-hour interrogation in the police station without an attorney present, Miranda had been induced to write his confession. The confession was used in the trial, and Miranda was convicted and sentenced to twenty to thirty years in prison for each offense. On appeal, the Supreme Court of Arizona ruled that the conviction should stand, noting that the suspect did not ask for an attorney.

The United States Supreme Court reversed the Arizona court decision, citing as unacceptable the methods used by the police to obtain confessions: not the possibility of physical violence—the legendary "third degree," which even the police agreed was a bit excessive—but the psychological persuasion recommended by police manuals then in use. As the Supreme Court noted in its decision:

> To highlight the isolation and unfamiliar surroundings, the manuals instruct the police to display an air of confidence in the suspect's guilt and from outward appearance

to maintain only an interest in confirming certain details. The guilt of the subject is to be posited as a fact. The interrogator should direct his comments toward the reasons why the subject committed the act, rather than court failure by asking the subject whether he did it. . . . The officers are instructed to minimize the moral seriousness of the offense, to cast blame on the victim or on society. These tactics are designed to put the subject in a psychological state where his story is but an elaboration of what the police purport to know already—that he is guilty. Explanations to the contrary are dismissed and discouraged.

It was widely believed among police agencies that this new protection for the accused was going to make effective law enforcement difficult to the point of impossibility. But it has not worked out that way. Even when Ernesto Miranda was retried for rape without his confession, he was again found guilty.

There is an interesting gray line that a witness crosses when becoming a suspect. At some point along this line the Miranda rights must be read for a confession to be admissible in court. If a witnesses confesses before he or she has become enough of a suspect to have the Miranda rights read, the detectives must read these rights and then kindly ask the suspect to repeat the confession so it can be used in court.

The next responsibility of the detectives is to search the crime scene area to locate and collect evidence. To go beyond the immediate area of the body they need either a consent-to-search form signed by whomever legally controls the property—usually either the landlord or a tenant— or a search warrant. To apply for a warrant the detectives must specify the area they want to search, what they expect to find there, and the probable cause—the importance of the sought-after material to the developing case and just why it is expected to be found there. The warrant is issued by a judge and can only be given to sworn peace officers; this is one of our rights contained in the Fourth Amendment to the Constitution, protecting us from unreasonable search and seizure. When the area to be searched is a crime scene, a judge will usually regard that fact as sufficient probable cause. The detectives will search for the weapon or other visible physical evidence that may be present. A more detailed search may be conducted by the forensic unit if there is need. In searching, the detectives should always work in pairs, one officer always within sight of the other. This makes it more difficult for the defendant's attorney to claim that one of the searchers planted any piece of evidence.

THE PRELIMINARY REPORT

As an example, here is the preliminary report of the Los Angeles detectives who answered the call on June 13, 1994, at the site where the bodies of Nicole Brown Simpson, the thirty-five-year-old ex-wife of former football player O. J. Simpson, and Ronald Goldman, a twenty-five-year-old waiter, were found. The homicide detectives attending were Tom Lange and Phil Vannatter.

County of Los Angeles, Investigator's Report, Department of Coroner

```
94-05135
Goldman, Ronald L.
FD 6-13-94
Homicide
LAPD Rob/Homi
See 94-05136
```

INFORMATION SOURCE:

```
Det(s) Lange and Vannatter (phone number)
At scene investigation
Louis Brown, father of decedent
```

LOCATION:

```
A private residence, 875 S. Bundy Dr., Los Angeles
```

INVESTIGATION:

```
94-05135 A 25-year-old male is the victim of an
  apparent homicide.
94-05136 A 35-year-old female is the victim of an
  apparent homicide.
The decedents appear to be the victims of sharp force
injuries.
```

STATEMENTS:

According to Det. Lang at about 0030 hrs. 6-13-94 a resident observed the dog belonging to the decedent 94-05136 wandering about the neighborhood. The resident reportedly walked the dog back to the above address and observed the decedents unresponsive. Emergency services were called to the scene and death was pronounced by Eng. 19 at 0045 hr.

The decedent 94-05136 was last known to be alive at about 2300 hrs. speaking to her mother on the telephone. Her mother had left her eyeglasses at a restaurant that evening and the decedent reportedly advised her mother that she should ask if an employee could bring them to her residence.

SCENE DESCRIPTION/BODY EXAMINATION

I arrived at the scene at 0905 hr. 6-13-94. The scene is the gated entrance to the decedent's (94-05136) residence. The decedent 94-05135 was observed at the north side of the entrance. He was seated in the dirt (garden area) slumped to his right side. His back was against a small tree stump and iron fence. He was dressed in blue jeans and a light colored cotton-type sweater. His clothes and face were stained with blood. Numerous sharp force injuries were observed at his neck, back, head and hands. Another wound was present at his left thigh area. Lividity was present and fixed, rigor mortis was fully established.

Lying near the decedent's (94-05135) right foot was a business size white envelope containing a pair of eyeglasses.

The decedent 94-05136 was lying at the foot of the stairs at the gate. She was in a fetal position on her left side, wearing a black dress, no shoes. Her legs were positioned under the stationery portion of the gate and her arms were bent at the elbow and close to her body. Coagulated and dried blood stained the walkway leading to the decedent. Paw prints were present at the side walk, consistent with a dog present/leaving the location. The gated area is several feet from the front entrance of the residence. Blood stains were present on the decedent's legs, arms and face. Examination revealed a large sharp force injury at the decedents neck, with smaller injuries just to the left side of the neck. Lividity was fixed and consistent with her position and rigor mortis was fully established.

```
EVIDENCE:

94-05135: Hair standards were taken and nail stan-
  dards could not be retrieved (nails too short.)

94-05136: Hair and nail standards taken as well as
  physical evidence by criminologist L. Mahanay (at
  the Forensic Science Center).

IDENTIFICATION/NOTIFICATION

94-05135: Identification was established at the
  scene by California Drivers License: A1347431.
  Notification was established to father, Fred
  Goldman, by this investigator.

94-05136: Identification was established at the
  scene by a passport. Notification was established
  to father, Louis Brown, by Det. Lange.

AUTOPSY NOTIFICATION

PLEASE CONTACT DET(S) LANGE AND VANNATTER (Phone
number) AT LEAST TWO HOURS PRIOR TO EXAMINATION.

Signed, C. Ratcliffe 203300, 6-13-94
```

[Note: "Eng. 19" is Engine 19 of the Emergency Services unit. "Lividity" and "rigor mortis" are means of determining time of death (see next chapter). The autopsy notification is to enable the detectives to be present at the autopsy.]

Many homicide detectives develop a "sixth sense" in recognizing a purposeful murder in what seems on the surface to be a random act of violence, an accidental death, or a suicide. If you ask a detective how he or she knew that a given case was not what it seemed, the response is often, "It just didn't feel right." When, early in the afternoon of Thursday, September 30, 1993, detectives Danny Caudill and Larry Reese of the Columbus, Ohio, homicide squad answered the call to investigate the death of thirty-year-old Greg Williams at Williams's townhouse, the feeling of wrongness was strong.

Williams, who had been shot twice in the chest and once in the right arm, had been taken to the emergency room at Riverside Methodist Hospitals, where he died at 2:42 P.M. Upon questioning, his twenty-three-year-old wife, Michele, said that she had been in the kitchen, "putting away nonperishable food and strategically placing my dishes," when she heard shots in the living room. She ran in to find Greg down, and the killer, a man twenty-five to thirty years old, rushing out the patio door. The man was wearing a dirty T-shirt, jeans, and a maintenance belt with tools attached.

Michele said she found Greg breathing loudly, with a sort of bloody bubble in his throat. She ran outside to scream for help and then came back in and cradled her dying husband in her arms. Michele, a sweet young blond who looked like every college man's dream date, told her story between sobs while being physically supported by a family friend to keep from collapsing completely. "You've got to catch that guy!" she told the detectives.

Throughout Michele and Greg's storybook romance, they had been the perfect couple, and still adored each other, as far as anyone could tell. They had just moved back from a year in Colorado, and the townhouse was still strewn with unpacked boxes. Greg was about to go into business with his brother, and all appeared to be content within the family.

But something about Michele—the way she told her story or perhaps the condition of the house—set off the alarm bells in the detectives' minds. It just didn't feel right. Michele and her mother were taken to the police station where Michele was to give her statement, while Caudill and Reese, acting on their hunch, searched the house. In a cardboard box in an upstairs bedroom, they found a laundry bag. And in the laundry bag, a .32-caliber revolver. In her purse, sitting in the kitchen, they found cartridges for the .32, as well as shell casings from the three rounds that had been fired.

At the police station Michele was being questioned by detective Dennis Graul, for whom she amplified her story about the stranger with the dirty T-shirt and the tool belt. But for Graul as well, her story just didn't seem right. He told her that he wanted to do a gunpowder residue test on her hands, one that would tell whether she had fired a pistol recently. She agreed, but he noted that when he left the room she began to scrub her palms frantically with cleansing tissue.

The test came back positive. With the gun, for which there was a record of Michele's purchase, the bullets, and the powder on her hands, the State of Ohio had no trouble getting a conviction.

The motive for her crime was never made clear. There was a $300,000 life insurance policy, but her husband was worth more than that alive.

Michele had had an interlude with a man in Colorado, which she evidently took more seriously than did he, but there was no indication that she took it seriously enough to kill over.

The detectives discovered that Michele had bought a book called *The Death Dealer's Manual* two months before the murder. It was apparently a handbook of sorts, but judging by the results, it was one that cannot be recommended.

Once the homicide detectives began looking for evidence, there was plenty to be found. But if the detectives hadn't learned to trust their instincts, they probably never would have bothered to search the upstairs bedroom or the purse of the loving wife, or thought to give her a gunpowder residue test.

Let us look now at what the homicide detectives found in the case of Godfrey Daniels, deceased:

The body of Mr. Daniels was lying on its back on the floor of his study. There was what appeared to be a bullet hole in the deceased's chest, and a pool of congealed blood had formed under the body in the area of the head and shoulder. Other stains of what could be blood were on the desk and on the floor near the door to the room. There was also what might be a blood stain on the inner doorknob of a second door, which led to a bathroom. A revolver lay about a foot from the deceased's left leg.

There was an overturned wastebasket and signs of a struggle or a hasty search, and it looked as though someone had gone through the desk drawers and file cabinet. But the apparent struggle could have happened if the decedent had shot himself and then, before passing out from the wound, changed his mind about committing suicide and struggled to reach the phone. The additional blood stains could have been put there quite innocently by the decedent's wife in trying to minister to her husband before she was sure he was dead.

Murder or suicide?

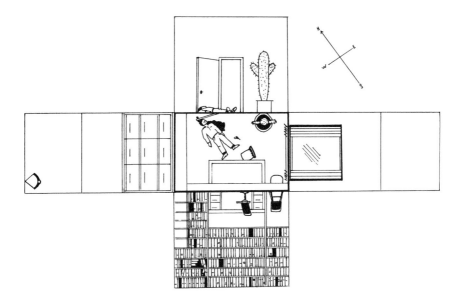

A METICULOUS EXPLODED DRAWING OF THE GODFREY
DANIELS CRIME SCENE AS IT WOULD BE DONE BY A
CRIMINALIST.

The detectives took Mrs. Cecilia Daniels's statement, in which she avowed that she left the house at 8:30 A.M. and spent the day at her store—Cecilia's Frocks, located in Wayne Manor, a large shopping mall in Richwood—until the store closed at 8:00 P.M. She then had dinner with a friend and came straight home, arriving, she estimated, at 9:15. About ten minutes after she arrived she went into her husband's study to speak to him and found him dead on the floor. She immediately dialed 911.

According to Mrs. Daniels, the last time she spoke to her husband was over the phone at about three o'clock that afternoon. He called to say he was expecting a client to drop in at about eight P.M., which is why, according to Mrs. Daniels, she had decided to eat out.

The detective who was questioning the wife noticed her reluctance to identify her dinner partner, a local businessman named William Batson. Was it merely a natural reluctance to involve him, or was there something in their relationship that she wished to conceal? A detective was dispatched to the home of William Batson to make sure that he verified Mrs. Daniels's story and to arrange for Mr. Batson to come down to the station the next day to have his fingerprints taken. If Mr. Batson agreed, then the prints almost certainly would not match any in the house. But if he refused, his story—and Mrs. Daniels's alibi—would be checked into more carefully.

The deceased was a prominent criminal attorney in Gotham City who defended many clients known to be nasty, brutish, amoral, and seriously emotionally disturbed. Sometimes all these features graced the same individual. Did this have anything to do with his death? And who was the mysterious visitor who, if the wife's story is to be believed, was supposed to see Daniels at eight o'clock?

The detectives went from door to door along the street questioning the Daniels's neighbors. Several of them reported seeing a strange man arriving at Daniels's house at around eight o'clock. The neighbor on the left is sure that it was a tall, thin man in a trench coat and a dark cap who slunk down the street at about ten minutes to eight. The neighbor two doors down on the right saw a stocky man with light hair and no hat in a blue or gray suit approach the Daniels' house a minute or so after eight o'clock. Could it be that Daniels was visited by two men, or is this merely two differing descriptions of the same man? As any freshman psychology student knows, it is not uncommon to get wildly divergent descriptions from multiple observers of the same event. Perhaps the forensic team could find some indications.

THE MEDICAL EXAMINER

The office of the medical examiner was called at the same time as was the homicide squad. Whether it had turned out to be murder, suicide, or accidental death, in all cases of unattended death or in cases where a death certificate cannot be issued by a competent physician, someone from the medical examiner's office must be called. They will examine the body where it lies to estimate the time and probable cause of death. Then they will take the body back to the morgue to perform an autopsy. We will peer over the shoulder of the Gotham City medical examiner in the next chapter.

THE FORENSIC UNIT

The size of the science crew can vary from a squad of six to eight specialists with a ton of equipment transported in their own special van, to one harried technician lugging a large equipment box. Their job is to locate, identify, preserve, and, where possible, remove for analysis all substances that may be clues to solving the crime. These technicians may either be sworn police officers or civilian employees of the police department. In any case, in a good unit they are all highly trained specialists who can carry an investigation from the discovery and lifting of a latent fingerprint or the recovery of a strand of hair or unidentified particle through the analysis of the constituent material to determine its significance in building the case against the perpetrator.

The forensic team sent to investigate the death of Godfrey Daniels consisted of two criminalists, a fairly average number. They worked according to a plan that they had developed over the time that they worked together; this assured that they did not overlook anything and that they would be able to recall all the pertinent facts should they be asked, on the witness stand, to describe in meticulous detail just how they happened to find whatever it was they found.

The duo began by photographing the scene, before the body was moved, from every angle that might prove useful. They then went over the area for fingerprints, looking in places that the assailant was likely to forget he had touched, like the bathroom sink or the underside of the desktop.

They took the water from the trap in the bathroom sink drain to test it for the presence of blood. They noted that the top desk drawer had been pulled out and gone through; on further inspection, they found that the other desk drawers had been similarly treated. The team bagged the gun for future examination and took samples from each of the blood stains, in some cases removing the entire stain, being careful to note where each had originated. They gathered and labeled other physical evidence such as hairs, fibers, and some cigarette butts found in an ashtray on the desk, and removed it all to the laboratory for analysis. Should the need arise, some exemplars would be sent to FBI laboratories or a specialized private facility.

Rather than waiting for daylight the forensic unit used powerful search-lights to examine the outside of the house, both front and back, for physical evidence, and found some likely footprints and tire tracks where a car had been parked. Near the car they found and carefully bagged a cigarette butt, which might have been discarded by the driver.

We will discuss their work in detail, along with the lab follow-up, after we look at the medical examiner's treatment of the deceased Mr. Daniels and examine some common problems with identification.

THREE

THE MEDICAL EXAMINER

The practice of medicine can be thought of as the organized effort of humanity to relieve pain and forestall the inevitability of death. Pathologists have stood on the front lines of this battle, facing death directly and probing its dark mysteries. Forensic pathologists, like spies in an enemy camp, seek out the secrets of the dead so the living can understand the manner of their demise and take appropriate action. Although discovering or confirming that a questionable death is a homicide is certainly one of the medical examiner's more important functions, the duties of the office cover a wide range beyond identifying a murder—from warning of a public health hazard to discovering the preventable cause of an accidental death. If citizens are dying from crack cocaine laced with cyanide, or from carbon monoxide from faulty space heaters, or from an outbreak of plague, it will probably be the medical examiner's office that discovers the threat and warns the public.

The office of chief medical examiner in Gotham City, as in many cities and counties in the United States, is a civil service position that has replaced the elective office of coroner. The medical examiners on staff, like their chief, must be trained, certified pathologists and by law must be notified in any cases of unusual or suspicious death, cases where the cause of death cannot reasonably be determined, or cases where there is no attending physician to issue a death certificate.

QUESTIONABLE DEATHS

According to the Office of Chief Medical Examiner of the City of New York, the medical examiner has jurisdiction over deaths occurring under the following circumstances:

- All forms of criminal violence or from an unlawful act or criminal neglect.
- All accidents (motor vehicle, industrial, home, public place, etc.).
- All suicides.
- All deaths that are caused or contributed to by drug and/or chemical overdose or poisoning.
- Sudden death of a person in apparent good health.
- Deaths which occur unattended by a physician and where no physician can be found to certify the cause of death. In this context, "unattended by a physician" shall mean not treated by a physician within thirty-one days immediately preceding death.
- Deaths of all persons in legal detention, jails, or police custody. This category also includes any prisoner who is a patient in a hospital, regardless of the duration of hospital confinement.
- Deaths which occur during diagnostic or therapeutic procedures or from complications of such procedures.
- When a fetus is born dead in the absence of a physician or midwife. Stillbirths in the hospital need not be reported to the Office of Chief Medical Examiner unless

there is a history of maternal trauma or drug abuse or the case has some other unusual or suspicious circumstance. Neonatal deaths from prematurity and its complications must be reported if the premature delivery was caused by maternal trauma or drug abuse.

- Deaths due to disease, injury, or toxic agent resulting from employment.
- When there is an intent to cremate or dispose of a body in any fashion other than interment in a cemetery.
- Dead bodies brought into the city without proper medical certification.
- Deaths which occur in any suspicious or unusual manner.

There are still many places around the country where the doctors who are called in to examine cases of unnatural death are not trained in forensic pathology, as many medical schools still feel that the subject is not worthy of the students' time. As Marshall Houts points out in his book *Where Death Delights*:

Only the barest percentage of medical students who graduate in the United States today ever get sufficient exposure to forensic medicine to even know what the subject covers.

Yet these are the men who are called upon . . . to determine whether a bullet wound is a wound of entrance or a wound of exit; whether bruises about a deceased's neck are consistent or inconsistent with some police officer's theory of manual strangulation; whether a burned body was dead or alive at the time of the fire; whether a newborn infant found in a garbage can ever breathed or was stillborn; whether a body found submerged in water drowned or was dead before it was thrown into the water; whether cuts and other marks on a body are consistent or inconsistent with a theory of suicide; whether death from a heart attack occurred before an automobile accident and caused the accident, or whether the accident occurred first and caused the heart attack . . .

THE CORONER

Coroners, a holdover from British criminal law, are the oldest known court officers, the position having been institutionalized in the time of Richard the Lion-Hearted. The office of *coronae custodium regis*, "keeper of the king's pleas," was established as a sort of tax collector to raise money for King Richard's ransom after he was captured by Leopold of Austria. Effective methods of taxation take on a life of their own, and so the office is with us yet, although somewhere along the way it mercifully lost its tax-collection function.

The relationship between coroners and crime was established early. Part of the coroner's job was to keep track of convicted felons and, after they were hanged, drawn and quartered, pressed by heavy stones, burned at the stake, or otherwise reprimanded—almost every felony was a capital offense in those days—seeing that the deceased felon's property was properly confiscated in the name of the king.

The office was brought to America at a time when its functions and personnel were not highly regarded in Britain. Here as there, the major function of the office had devolved into the investigation of unusual deaths. But there were no professional qualifications for holding the post of coroner, which was an elective office in the United States. The coroner—sometimes sitting as a single judge, sometimes with the aid of a coroner's jury—would hold a court proceeding known as an *inquest* or a *post mortem* to determine whether a crime had been committed and if there was probable cause to say that a certain person had committed the crime. The decisions were binding on the victim, but not on the suspect (if any); that is, the coroner's findings could be used in settling estates or insurance questions, but it would take an indictment by a grand jury or preliminary hearing before a trial judge to bring someone to trial on a felony charge.

In many places the job of coroner would go to the local mortician, as he was the only one with facilities for handling dead bodies. In other areas the job became blatantly corrupt and political. In New York City in the nineteenth century, coroners were paid a set fee per inquest, so they would often hold three or four inquests over the same body. Others let it be known that for an extra ten dollars they would change the official cause of death from suicide to accidental death—many families had strong moral feelings about suicides, and many insurance companies had (and still have) restrictive clauses about collecting on a suicide's life insurance policy. It was also reported that there were some particularly venal coroners who, for fifty dollars, would change a finding of homicide to accidental death, enabling miscreants to literally get away with murder.

The coroner's court was held in the manner of the coroner's choosing; witnesses had no right to have an attorney present and might be forced to answer questions that would be forbidden in a formal court of law. The flaws in the system were forcibly brought to the attention of the citizens of Greater New York in 1897, when a Brooklyn coroner was found to have had the body of a drowned man dragged from place to place along the East River waterfront, holding an inquest over the body at each new location. He billed the city for ten thousand dollars in fees, but the morgue reported only one body. The next year, when Brooklyn, Manhattan, and the other three boroughs united officially to form New York City, they also did away with the coroner's fee system, substituting a salaried office. Twenty years later, in 1918, the City of New York did away with the office of coroner entirely, replacing it with the medical examiner.

(One of the more interesting coroner's jury decisions came shortly before the office was abolished. A husky, six-foot businessman named Murray Hall died in bed. The coroner's physician determined that the cause of death had been a heart attack and that the "businessman's" gender was female, a fact that even Hall's niece, who lived in the same apartment, had been unaware of. The jury's verdict: "We find that Murray Hall came to his death by natural causes. He was a lady.")

Dr. Milton Helpern, who served with distinction as the Chief Medical Examiner of the City of New York for many years, explained the difference between coroner and medical examiner thus:

> The medical examiner must be a doctor of medicine with special training and experience in the field of pathology. The coroner is not required to have any specialized training or professional qualifications. He may be, and often is, a funeral director or mortician, a furniture dealer, a barber, or a merchant. Sometimes he is the elected sheriff of a county.
>
> The coroner system is gradually being abolished throughout the rest of the United States, with coroners being replaced by medical examiners. As in many other jurisdictions in the United States, Los Angeles has retained the title of coroner, but the office is filled by a qualified medical examiner. In some locales the office of coroner is still elective and no qualifications exist save the ability to be elected, but the coroner is required to hire qualified forensic pathologists to conduct the autopsies and other medico-legal inquiries.

Fortunately, Gotham City's chief medical examiner has a well-trained staff. Whenever possible in a suspected homicide and when the caseload permits, a medical examiner will be sent to the death scene to gather the medical evidence directly prior to performing the autopsy. The medical examiners who were dispatched to the scene of Godfrey Daniels's murder were to determine, as best they could, the approximate cause and time of death. They did this by questioning the witnesses, taking note of the surroundings, and examining the body. The three factors most useful in determining the time of death are *rigor mortis*, the rigidity that comes and goes shortly after death; *livor mortis*, the discoloration of the skin caused by the settling of the red cells of the blood due to gravity; and *algor mortis*, the gradual cooling off of the body.

Rigor mortis begins about two hours after death, as the body chemistry slowly changes from alkaline to acid. The muscles, which were completely relaxed at death, begin to stiffen. The process usually appears first in the eyelids and the muscles of the face and then spreads to the jaw, the arms, the trunk, and the legs, in that order. An arm or leg in the grip of rigor is hard and stiffly held in position; a body in full rigor is stiff as a plank. The condition reaches a peak in about twelve hours and lasts from twelve to forty-eight hours. Then, as the chemistry of death continues and the body changes once more from acid back to alkaline, rigor begins to pass, disappearing in the order that it arrived, clearing first from the face, and then the jaw, the arms, the trunk, and the legs.

In some very rare cases of instantaneous violent death a condition known as *cadaveric spasm* occurs, in which the body appears to go into rigor at the instant of death. In these cases anything the corpse was clutching at the time of death—a gun, a note, a patch of his assailant's hair—will be held rigidly for hours until the condition passes. There is some dispute as to whether this is a form of rigor mortis or not, but its effect is much the same. After it passes, normal rigor will set in.

Livor mortis, also known as post-mortem lividity, occurs when, following death, the red cells of the blood gradually settle out of the serum and gather at the lowest part of the body. The first signs begin to show after about two hours, and lividity is fixed after about eight hours, when the red cells begin to break down and migrate out of the capillaries and into the surrounding muscle. Thereafter, no matter how the body is moved, the characteristic red markings stay where they formed. Lividity that appears in the wrong place—any place but the lowest points on the body—is a sure sign that the body has been moved since death.

Algor mortis, the temperature of death, allows an investigator to estimate how long the body has been dead by measuring its internal temperature. At the moment of death the person, unless he or she died of a fever, had a body temperature of approximately 98.6 degrees Fahrenheit/37 degrees Celsius (though once regarded as an absolute, it is now recognized that some people have normal body temperatures as much as two degrees above or below the norm). The temperature of the body then goes down at the rate of about one degree an hour, depending upon external temperature and the victim's body weight, among other things.

By using these gauges the Gotham City assistant medical examiners concluded that attorney Daniels had been killed about three hours before they arrived, give or take half an hour, which would put the approximate time of death between 7:30 and 8:30 P.M., a time when the wife was not home and during which the deceased had an appointment with a mysterious caller. The examiners warned the detectives, however, that this preliminary conclusion about the time of death was extremely tentative and could not be relied on. Unknown factors may have altered the values of any of their three indicators and could drastically throw off their conclusions.

Since the crime scene contained signs of a struggle, it was possible that hair or skin from Daniels's assailant remained under his fingernails. Therefore plastic bags were placed around the victim's hands and tied at his wrists. The examiners then carefully placed the body into a plastic zipper bag and removed it to the morgue to be autopsied.

When a body arrives at the medical examiners' facility it must be positively identified by a family member or close friend. A special area is set aside for viewing the body, which is usually behind glass in another room to lessen the impact on a spouse or close relative. (In New York City, identification of a Polaroid photograph especially taken for this purpose is legally sufficient.) If there is no one around to identify the corpse, it will be photographed and fingerprinted by the Medical Examiner's Unit of the New York City Police Department and the fingerprints will be sent to different agencies for identification.

It is the job of the pathologist in an autopsy to determine both the identity of the corpse and the exact cause of death. Nothing can be taken for granted. Just because the body of Mr. Daniels was brought in with a bullet hole in it, it still remained to be established that he died of the gunshot wound. He might have been dead when the shot was fired. He might have been wounded by the bullet and then bashed over the head with a blunt object. The hole in the body might not even be a bullet hole; it might have been done with an ice ax or a hatpin or a pointed stick.

On the other hand, the death might be as initially represented but the body might not be that of Mr. Daniels. When the medical examiner puts the name of the deceased at the top of the death certificate she had better be pretty sure that she is declaring the right person to be dead.

If at all possible at least one of the homicide detectives will be present at the autopsy. This serves several purposes: The detective can ask whatever questions occur to him during the course of the autopsy and get the answer immediately and in language he can understand. The detective can testify in court as to the results of the autopsy from his own firsthand knowledge, if the medical facts of the case are not complicated enough to require the testimony of the medical examiner. Since the detective will probably have to testify anyway, this takes some of the burden off the medical examiner's office, which is always pressed for time for things such as court appearances.

On the other hand, if it is a politically important case, both the detective working the case and a representative of the District Attorney's office will possibly be present, and the medical examiner can be assured she will be required to testify. In New York City it is now policy for two medical examiners to be present at each autopsy, so that one can verify the other's findings if necessary.

Michael M. Baden, former chief medical examiner for New York City, points out in his book *Confessions of a Medical Examiner*:

> It takes about two hours to do an uncomplicated autopsy on a person who died of a stroke or a heart attack. Bullet wounds take longer. Mafia killings always take more time because of the number of bullet holes. We have to check each injury to see whether it contributed to the death.

When the defunct Mr. Daniels arrived at the morgue, he was taken into one of the autopsy rooms and placed on the examination table. His clothes were carefully examined to see what information they could contribute to the search for the cause of death. For example, it was established that the bullet hole in his chest aligns with the bullet holes in his shirt and jacket. The angle at which they line up may give an indication of Mr. Daniels's posture at the moment he was shot. Clothing rides differently on the body when the subject is standing, sitting, kneeling, twisting around, or bending over. And, of course, if the holes failed to line up at all, then we know that the corpse was dressed, or redressed, after death. Thus the investigation would take an unexpected twist.

OFFICE OF CHIEF MEDICAL EXAMINER
CITY OF NEW YORK

AUTOPSY NOTES

NAME OF DECEASED:_____ M.E.#_____-_____-_____

WD/WN:_____ HEIGHT:___FT___IN WEIGHT:_____LB SKIN COLOR:_____ ♂ / ♀ AGE:_____

HAIR: TXTR_____ CLR_____ ___IN M___IN B___IN EYES: IRIDES_____ CONJ_____ TEETH/ORAL_____

TORSO: ANT_____ POST_____ EXTREMITIES: UPPER_____ LOWER_____ GENITALIA:_____

RIGOR MORTIS:_____ LIVOR MORTIS: F/B_____ TEMPERATURE:_____

SCARS:

TATTOOS:

CLOTHING:

THERAPEUTIC PROCEDURES:

INJURIES:

HEAD
BRAIN _____ GM
NECK
CAVITIES _____
HEART _____ GM
  L.V. _____ CM
R-LUNG _____ GM
L-LUNG _____ GM
LIVER _____ GM   DIAGNOSES:
  BILE _____ ML
PANCREAS   _____
SPLEEN _____ GM
  LYMPH NODES   _____
  THYMUS: Y/N
R-KIDNEY _____ GM   _____
L-KIDNEY _____ GM
  URINE _____ ML   _____
GONADS
ENDOCRINE   _____
DIGESTIVE TRACT
  GASTRIC _____ ML   _____
  APP: Y/N
MUSC-SKEL   _____

EXAMINED BY: _____M.D.   DATE:_____ /_____ / ____

STANDARD AUTOPSY FORM (FRONT AND BACK) USED BY
THE OFFICE OF CHIEF MEDICAL EXAMINER, CITY OF NEW
YORK.

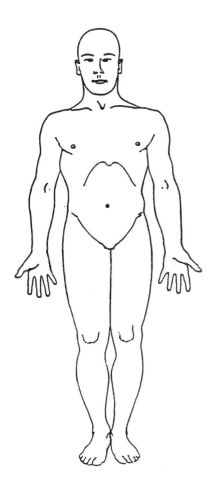 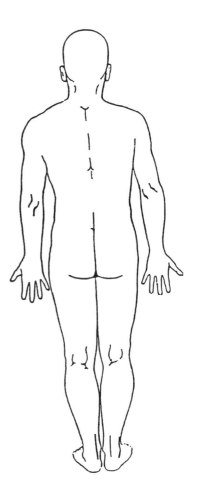

The medical examiner performed the autopsy in the modern, up-to-date facility at the Gotham City morgue, where every aid to accuracy was built in. A microphone was placed in proximity to the autopsy table so that she could murmur her findings into a tape recorder to be transcribed later. Her first words, established by custom, echoed the opening of the Catholic sacrament of Holy Communion: *Hoc es Corpus . . .*

"This is the body," the medical examiner intoned into her microphone, "of a well-developed, well-nourished, white male, measuring five feet, eleven inches in height and weighing approximately two hundred and ten pounds. He is wearing . . ."

The body was photographed before it was undressed, and then the clothes were removed by the medical examiner, aided by technicians wearing rubber gloves so as not to contaminate any evidence present. The clothing was then bagged and tagged for further study.

The now-naked body had a toe-tag put around the big toe so it wouldn't be confused with any other body at any stage of the autopsy procedure. It was then photographed once again, from whichever angles were deemed useful, and the camera (and perhaps the photographer) remained available throughout the autopsy so that photographs could be taken of any abnormality discovered at any part of the procedure. Of course in many cases the pathologist is his own photographer.

PICTURES

Autopsy pictures can be more than useful—they can be critical in answering questions that might not occur until years after the autopsy has been completed. And the process of taking photographs so that they illustrate clearly what needs to be seen is a specialized skill in itself. When the body of President John Kennedy was autopsied after his assassination, the autopsy pathologist, Dr. James Humes, a navy commander, wrote in the autopsy report: "The complexity of these fractures and the fragments thus produced tax satisfactory verbal description and are better appreciated in photographs and roentgenograms [x-ray pictures] which are prepared." Unfortunately for posterity, an officious FBI agent decided that the corpsman who was trained to take the pictures had no "clearance" to be at the autopsy. What sort of clearance he was required to have is not known.

The remaining photographer, an FBI man who did have clearance, had no experience in photographing gunshot wounds. As Dr. Michael M. Baden explains in his book *Unnatural Death*:

> His pictures showed it. A proper photograph would have shown the injury first as it was and then cleaned off, next to a ruler to give perspective on its size and position in the body. None of his pictures clearly defined the entrance or exit wounds. The photographs of the body's interior were out of focus. You have to know at what level you want to shoot—the chest is deep. He didn't take pictures of any internal organs. These are the pictures Humes proposed to rely on, his own descriptive powers having failed him.

The lack of adequate autopsy photographs is at least part of the reason why the death of President Kennedy has remained a mystery, and why the various conspiracy theories refuse to die.

Then the epidermis, or outer skin layer, of Mr. Daniels was carefully examined for cuts, bruises, wounds, puncture marks, scars, and any other abnormalities that might be present. If there were any reason to suspect—or to rule out—drug use or other possible reasons for injections, the medical examiner would have gone over the body with a magnifying glass, looking for fresh puncture marks. And since hypodermic injection sites heal quickly and usually disappear within forty-eight hours, any injection marks found would be comparatively fresh.

The medical examiner examined the bullet hole and determined that it was an entrance wound. By the burn marks around it he could tell that the bullet was fired from close range. The detective watching the autopsy made a note of this; he would have the forensic laboratory test the skin and the shirt around the bullet hole for powder residues. He was already thinking of his presentation in court, and a laboratory report showing powder residue would impress a jury more than the medical examiner's opinion that the area of skin surrounding the wound showed burn marks.

The medical examiner checked the fingernails for rips or tears and took scrapings from under the nails. If Daniels fought his assailant at all there might have been some sign under his fingernails. In this case, unfortunately, the nail scrapings were devoid of useful material.

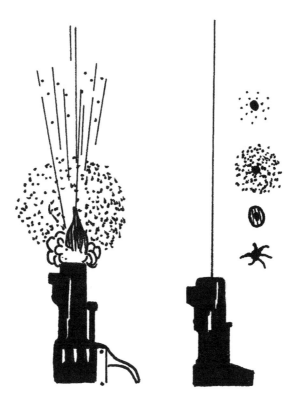

IN ADDITION TO THE BULLET, A FIRED GUN ALSO EX-
PELS GAS AND PARTICLES OF UNBURNED PROPELLANT,
WHICH WILL LEAVE A DISTINCTIVE PATTERN ON A CLOSE
TARGET.

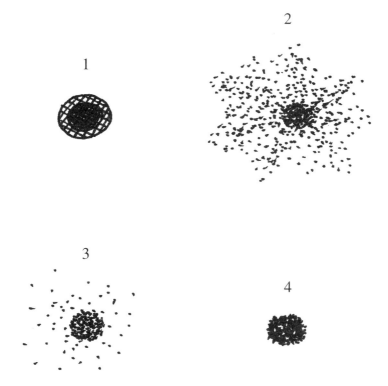

PATTERN OF BURN MARKS: 1. POINT-BLANK; 2. CLOSE
RANGE (UP TO TWO FEET); 3. MEDIUM CLOSE (UP TO
FOUR FEET); 4. DISTANT.

A sample of the corpse's blood was taken for typing. Since there were numerous blood stains at the scene of the crime, it might be useful to know whether or not they are the victim's.

The medical examiner turned the body over to look for an exit wound. Finding none, she had the body x-rayed to have a clear idea of where to search for the bullet. Bullets can take strange paths through the body, and often their track closes behind them, making them hard to trace. (A modern autopsy room will have the x-ray machine and a darkroom for developing the x-ray film conveniently located nearby.) During the course of the autopsy the fatal bullet was recovered from inside the chest cavity and turned over to the homicide detective.

After the surface examination the internals were considered. The standard autopsy incision is in the shape of a Y—a cut from each shoulder meeting at the pit of the stomach and then continued down and through the pelvis. Even in a case where the cause of death seems evident, like that of Mr. Daniels, the internal organs—heart, lungs, spleen, liver, and so on—are removed and physically examined for abnormality or damage. They are weighed, and tissue samples are removed and carefully saved for chemical and toxicological analysis. The stomach is also removed and its contents examined and samples taken. If any food is present, and it can be determined when and what the victim last ate, then a fairly precise time of death can be determined by how much digestion has proceeded between the meal and the death.

Any fluid in the thoracic (chest) cavity or other body cavities is siphoned off and saved for analysis. Urine present in the bladder will also be aspirated and sent off for analysis. Most drugs that may be present in the victim can be detected in the urine.

Examination of the head is usually one of the last things done. The face is examined for minute wounds, the skull is examined for fractures, and the area around the eyes is examined for pinpoint hemorrhages called *petechiae*, which appear in cases of strangulation or hanging. The skin of the head is sliced across the top of the scalp, and a flap is pulled down in front of the face to allow the skull to be sawed open and the brain removed for examination. It is a gruesome and disturbing sight if you are not used to it, but when the section of skull is replaced and the skin flap pulled back into place, the face and head can be prepared for the funeral so that the damage is invisible to the viewer.

It may seem that when the cause of death is obvious—a gunshot or drowning, for example—the complex and thorough procedures of the medical examiner are a waste of time. But many times it has been shown that the seemingly obvious cause of death is only a contributing factor, or indeed is not the true cause at all. People have been found to have been shot or stabbed when there was no visible entrance wound.

If the body was found in the water but there is no water found in the lungs or stomach, then the victim was most likely dead upon entering the water. If the body was found in the ocean but the water found in the lungs is fresh water, then there is cause for suspicion regarding the events between death and the body's discovery.

A similar process of discovery applies to bodies found in or around the scene of a fire. If there are carbon particles in the lungs, then the victim may have died in the fire, but if there are no such particles, then the victim died before the fire started—or died elsewhere and was placed in the fire.

When the physical part of the autopsy has been completed, the internal organs, minus the tissue samples, will be placed back in the body cavity, and the body will be sewn back together. The skin flap on the head will be replaced, and the body will be put into storage. The chemical and biological tests on the tissue samples can take weeks to complete, and they may be done at laboratories thousands of miles from the autopsy site. When the cause of death has been determined, a death certificate will be issued and, unless there is some reason to act otherwise, the body will be released to the family.

FOUR

THE GUN

Please do not shoot the pianist. He is doing his best.

— OSCAR WILDE

The gun found on the floor at the feet of the defunct Mr. Daniels was a .38-caliber Colt revolver of respectable age, serial number Y136453, which had six shells in the cylinder, one of which had been fired. It was picked up very carefully by sliding a pen through the trigger guard (rather than down the barrel, despite the way they do it in movies; valuable information can be obliterated by carelessly sticking something down the barrel of a suspect firearm). The fresh odor of burned gunpowder, easily detectable by smelling the barrel, indicated to the criminalists that the firing had been recent. A check of the Gotham City firearms records showed that it was registered to Mr. Godfrey Daniels, and he had owned it for five years, buying it used from a local gun dealer. Fingerprints were found on the barrel, the cylinder, and several of the shells, but they all proved to be those of the deceased. A GSR (gunshot residue) test on the deceased's hands indicated that he had recently fired a weapon with his right hand.

The bullet removed from the body of Mr. Daniels was a .32-caliber, which would seem to indicate that Mr. Daniels did not shoot himself. He certainly did not shoot himself with the gun found at the scene. So the question is, whom or what did he shoot? And what happened to the bullet? And, of equal interest and more immediate importance, who shot him?

Because of the ubiquitousness of handguns in many areas of the United States, and the common confusion of propinquity with knowledge, many people in this country consider themselves to be firearms experts. Most of them are mistaken. The majority of those who handle guns regularly, including police officers, know little if anything about the forensics of firearms. Judge Charles W. Fricke, in his book *Criminal Investigation*, tells of a murder case tried in his court where the autopsy surgeon described the bullet recovered from the decedent's body as a .22 short. The police investigators neglected to enter into evidence the cluster of .22-long cartridge cases they had found near the body. It wasn't until after the defendant had been acquitted that someone pointed out to the investigators, and to the autopsy surgeon, that although the cartridges are different, the bullet slugs for the .22 long and the .22 short are identical.

The term ballistics comes from the Latin *ballista*, a sort of giant crossbow. It was originally the study of missiles in flight, a subject of great interest to the military, who wanted to be able to tell where the missiles would land. By extension the term has come to refer to firearms, and a forensic ballistics expert is someone who is knowledgeable in all facets of the study of firearms.

The questions that may be asked of a ballistics or firearms expert are: What sort of weapon is this? From where might it have come? What sort of projectile does it fire? What sort of projectile is this? What sort of weapon was it fired from? Is this weapon the actual one the projectile was fired from? From what distance was it fired? Was the shooting accidental or deliberate?

OF TIME AND THE GUN

The first guns were little more than tubes with a large hole bored lengthwise through one end and a tiny hole drilled at right angles at the other. The large hole went deep into the tube; into this was packed the charge of gunpowder followed by the projectile, usually a metal ball. The small hole was extended to reach the big hole at the point where the gunpowder was located. The tube was called the barrel, the big hole was the bore, and the little hole was the vent or touch-hole. When the gun was loaded a flame was applied to the vent, which set off the gunpowder, which expanded rapidly and shoved the projectile out the front end, called the muzzle. Since the projectile was inserted into the same hole it subsequently came out of, these guns were called muzzle-loaders.

Cannons were probably first used at the Battle of Crécy in 1346; it took a couple of centuries to get them small enough for a person to carry. The first handguns date to the early sixteenth century. They looked like miniature cannons, were heavy and slow to load, and many were designed to double as clubs should the enemy get too close before reloading had been completed.

For the first three hundred years of the gun's development, its improvements came in metallurgy—making the barrel lighter and less inclined to blow up—and in devising ways to get the spark to the vent hole.

The trigger was first developed as the lower end of an S-shaped device called the *serpentin*, the top of which held a slow-burning match, or fuse. The serpentin was hinged in the middle, and when the bottom was pulled the match was forced against a small cup which held priming powder, called the flash pan. If everything went right, the powder went off, sending a spark down the vent and igniting the main charge. But it was a chancy procedure. Sometimes the powder in the pan went off without setting off the charge below. From this phenomenon we get the expression "a flash in the pan."

The serpentin evolved into the matchlock, which accomplished the same task in a more complicated manner, and then the wheel-lock, which rotated a piece of steel next to a flint to send sparks into the pan. The next technological advance, the flintlock, had a sort of hammer and a cover on the pan to keep the powder dry.

FIFTEENTH-CENTURY FOOT SOLDIER FIRING AN
ARQUEBUS, THE PRECURSOR OF ALL MODERN HAND
WEAPONS. THE GUN, ESSENTIALLY A BARREL WITH
A TOUCH-HOLE AT THE CLOSED END TO SET OFF THE
GUNPOWDER, WAS HARD TO LOAD, UNRELIABLE TO
FIRE, AND LACKED THE RANGE, ACCURACY, AND
RAPIDITY OF FIRE OF A LONG BOW. BUT IT WAS EASY
TO TEACH AND THE NOISE FRIGHTENED THE ENEMY.

For the first few hundred years of their use, handguns were regarded as unsporting in battle. Lord Montluc, a French noble who served under Francis I (1515–1547), put it this way:

I . . . have seen brave and valiant men killed with it in such sad numbers, and it generally happened that they were struck down to the ground by those abominable bullets, which had been discharged by cowardly and base knaves, who would never have dared to have met true soldiers face to face and hand to hand. All this is very clearly one of those artifices which the devil employs to induce us human beings to kill one another.

The breach-loading gun became possible in the mid-eighteenth century, when metallurgical skills and machine tolerances became fine enough to assure that the breech (the area at the rear holding the powder charge) wouldn't blow up when the weapon was fired. In the nineteenth century the percussion cap was developed, replacing the flash pan and giving a greater assurance that the weapon would actually fire. This hastened the development of various schemes for holding multiple charges in the breach so the weapon could be fired several times without reloading. Later in the nineteenth century, the primer, powder charge, and ball were all wrapped together in one package, called a cartridge, and the revolving cylinder was perfected—by Samuel Colt among other people. The modern hand weapon was born.

The first person to cut spiral grooves down the length of the inside of a gun barrel is believed to have been Gaspard Kollner, a fifteenth-century Viennese gunmaker. This technique is known as "rifling" and is done to impart a spin to the projectile. It had been known since the days of the crossbow that a spinning projectile flew straighter and was less inclined to tumble in flight. This made rifled firearms (rifles) much more accurate than smoothbores (muskets). By the middle of the nineteenth century, techniques of mechanical bore-cutting had progressed to the point where rifling could be done cheaply, and rifles began replacing muskets in the world's armies. Shotguns, intended to fire a cluster of small "shot" instead of a solid slug, remained smoothbore.

The next great advance was the automatic rifle or pistol, which loaded a magazine full of shells and used the power of the expanding gases that drove the bullet forward to also drive an ejection and reloading mechanism at the breach of the gun. Semi-automatics would perform this mechanical ballet each time the trigger was pulled, whereas fully automatic "machine guns" would continue to fire once the trigger was pulled until it was released or the magazine was empty.

Luckily for the forensic scientist, each advance in gun design made it easier to retrieve information from the ballistics evidence at a crime scene: Smoothbore muskets left no characteristic markings on the bullet and muzzle-loaders left no hammer indentation on the shell, but breach-loading rifles or pistols left both. Revolvers took their shell casings away with them, whereas automatics spilled their seed on the ground for criminalists to find.

The primary identification of a gun is its caliber, maker, and type, as in a .38-caliber Colt revolver. The caliber is the measure of the diameter of the bullet in hundredths of an inch, unless it's a European caliber, in which case the measurement is in millimeters (mm). Many of the caliber designations in common use are nominal (which means we've all agreed to call them that) and they're pretty close, but not exact. The actual width of a .32-caliber automatic bullet, for example, is 0.3125 inch; the .38 Colt is actually 0.359 inch. There is even variance within the same supposed caliber number, depending on the gun the bullet is designed for: The .44 Smith & Wesson Special cartridge is actually 0.431 inch, while the .44 Winchester is 0.4255 inch.

Bullets designated one caliber can sometimes be fired from a gun of a different, but similar caliber. Both Colt and Smith & Wesson manufacture their .45-caliber revolvers so that ammunition designed for the .45 automatic can be used in them as well. Standard European calibers are sometimes close enough to American calibers to enable cross-usage: .32-caliber revolvers can handle 7.65mm cartridges, and .25-caliber revolvers can fire 6.35mm shells.

To add to the confusion, in an effort to fool the police or merely because he was out of the proper ammunition, a felon may have wrapped paper around a cartridge to fit it into a chamber designed for a larger caliber shell, making weapon and bullet caliber that much harder to identify.

The examination of a weapon found at a crime scene may answer many interesting questions: Are there any fingerprints on it, and to whom do they belong? If the weapon is loaded, are there any fingerprints on the cartridges? Is it the same caliber as the bullet removed from the victim? Are the cartridges remaining in the weapon of the same type as the one in the victim or elsewhere at the crime scene? If it is a revolver or single-shot pistol, are there any expended shell casings still in the weapon? If so, do they match the type of bullet that was fired?

OOPS

When the police entered the house of Robert and Barbara Parks on February 18, 1950, they found Robert, a thirty-eight-year-old retired army captain, in the bedroom, dead from a gunshot wound. He was lying on the floor near the door to the dining room, with a bullet hole in his right side. The autopsy established that the bullet had passed from right to left through his chest and stopped just on the far side of his heart.

Parks's wife, Barbara, was twelve years younger than the captain, and the couple had a history of violent quarrels. She was also known to have telephoned someone in San Francisco a couple of weeks before, asking for a one-way bus ticket so she could leave her husband.

When the police found Barbara, she was hysterical. Her story was that she had been in the kitchen when she heard a shot. Racing into the bedroom, she found her husband standing by the door. He said, "Honey, the gun backfired," and then fell dead.

The murder weapon, an automatic pistol, was lying against the far wall of the dining room, with one shot fired. The cartridge case had jammed in the ejection port. Forensic investigation showed that Parks could not have been holding the gun himself when it was fired, regardless of how it could have been thrown across the room.

Barbara Parks was taken to Luray, the nearest reasonably sized town, and put in jail.

The investigators had two questions to answer before winding up the case. One was why Mrs. Parks would tell such an improbable story when so many other more plausible tales were available to her: for example, self-defense, or she thought he was a burglar, or he was teaching her how to shoot it when it went off by accident. The other question was how did the brown-painted hot-air grill in the doorway between the dining room and the bedroom get a brand-new dent on it that chipped the paint away down to the metal?

The detectives wrapped up the evidence; gun, bullet, cartridge case, and hot-air grill were sent to the FBI Crime Laboratory. The FBI technicians verified that the bullet that killed Captain Parks had been fired from that gun, as had the cartridge, and that the gun had been fired from farther away than Parks could have held it.

But what of the dent in the hot-air grill? The technicians matched it with two points on the slide and hammer of the automatic, and searched for and found microscopic bits of brown paint from the grill on those spots on the gun. In reconstructing the scene they found that if the weapon had discharged as it struck the grill, the bullet would have hit Parks just where it actually did. Then how did it get all the way across the room? The only scenario that fit was that Captain Parks, a man with a violent temper, threw the gun away from him in a fit, it hit the grill and fired, the bullet hit Parks, the cartridge jammed when the slide was obstructed in its travel by the heating grill, and then the gun bounced across the dining room.

A firearms expert from the FBI Crime Laboratory came to Virginia to testify to these findings. The judge ruled that Parks's death was an accident. Barbara Parks's seemingly unbelievable story was true. She was released from jail and went home.

Examination of the interior of the barrel of a discovered weapon can be instructive. A layer of dust or rust particles or a spider web in the barrel is a good indication that it has not been fired recently. A deposit of gunpowder residue indicates that the weapon has not been cleaned since it was last fired, but the deposit will not in itself divulge how long ago that happened. If the gun in question was fired close to the victim, particles of blood, flesh, or fabric which ejected from the wound may be found in the barrel.

Identification of a fired bullet by class (caliber and type of casing) is not too difficult, if the bullet is still in reasonably good shape. The FBI Crime Laboratory and the laboratories of any fairly large police department will have comparison bullets to check against their exemplar. Bullets manufactured for the same caliber of weapon can vary in their jacket, composition, weight, and (although this can't be measured in a spent bullet) in the powder charge in the shell.

Confirming that a bullet was fired from a particular gun is made easier by the necessities of gun design. The barrels of all modern pistols and rifles (but not shotguns) are "rifled," that is, one or more spiral grooves are carved down the length of the barrel's interior (*see* "Of Time and the Gun," *p. 62*). When the weapon is fired the pressure causes the bullet to expand slightly to fill the grooves, which imparts a spin to the bullet, improving the accuracy of the gun and leaving the bullet with the impressions of these lands (the part of the bore that wasn't cut away) and grooves. This pattern makes it possible for the criminalist to distinguish the gun from which the bullet was fired, or at least to narrow down the number of possibilities.

The size and spacing of the lands and grooves and their direction and angle of twist is known for all commercial hand weapons. A class determination of the weapon used can often be made when the fired bullet is recovered in good condition. That is, the criminalist can say with some assurance: "This is a 115-grain 9mm bullet, manufactured by Winchester and probably fired from a Glock Model 19." There are many possible differences in the barrel markings. Most American gun makers use a right-hand twist, but Smith & Wesson uses a left-hand twist. The number of grooves cut into the barrel varies from four to eight, with six being the most common. But there are many manufacturers in the market today, each with several different models, a volume of weaponry that creates the need for the use of a fairly large crime laboratory to make the identification. Among the more respectable handgun manufacturers or importers today are Accu-Tek, American Arms, AMT, Astra, Auto-Ordnance, Baby Eagle, Beretta, Bersa Da Auto, Browning, Calico, Colt, Coonan, Davis, Dae Woo, EAA, FEG, Glock, Heckler & Koch, Intratec, Israel Military Industries, Jennings, L.A.R., Laserarms, Llama,

Lorcin, Mauser, Navy Arms, Norinco, Para-Ordnance, Phoenix Arms Co., Ruger, Sig-Sauer, Smith & Wesson, Springfield Inc., Star, Taurus, Walther, and Wildey. Each manufacturer produces anywhere from one to twenty or so different models in a variety of calibers, with prices on their weapons ranging from under $200 to over $1,200. Add to this the number of weapons no longer manufactured but still around—plus all the "Saturday night specials," handguns so cheaply made that they often don't carry a maker's mark—and the possible matches become vast.

Sometimes a bullet recovered from a crime scene will have no rifling marks. For example, solid slugs, made for shotguns, are in common use in some areas, as deer hunters are often required to use shotguns instead of rifles (a shotgun slug will not carry as far as a rifle bullet; therefore, if the hunter misses the deer, he has less chance of hitting another hunter). But if the bullet recovered has no rifling marks, yet is of a caliber usually fired through a rifled barrel, this is a good indication that it was fired from a homemade weapon, the sort that used to be called a "zip gun."

To go beyond the class identification and discover whether a given gun fired the bullet found at the crime scene (or in the body of the victim), the criminalist will fire a test bullet from the suspect gun into a box full of cotton waste or into a deep container of water to minimize damage to the bullet, and use a specially designed double-lensed comparison microscope to compare it with the crime-scene bullet. However, if the gun has been fired many times between the crime scene bullet and the test bullet, it may be difficult or impossible to confirm that it is the weapon that fired the crime scene bullet—every time a gun is fired, the barrel wears slightly, and the pattern it imposes on the bullet changes somewhat.

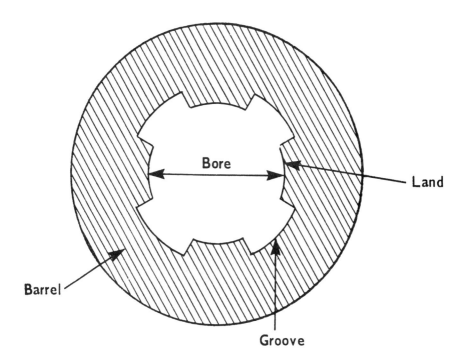

CROSS-SECTION OF THE MUZZLE OF A RIFLED BARREL.

There are several basic types of bullets made for different purposes, and each type presents a unique problem for the investigator. Most bullets are made entirely of lead or have a lead core covered by a steel jacket. A full-jacketed, or solid-nosed, bullet has a steel case that goes from the tip to the base of the slug, leaving the lead exposed only at the rear end that fits into the shell. A semijacketed, or soft-nosed, bullet reverses this, covering the entire base but leaving the soft lead point exposed. A type of bullet known as a hollow point takes this a step farther—it is constructed with a cavity behind the tip. Full-jacketed bullets tend to go through soft tissue or even a moderate amount of bone cleanly, leaving a small hole and doing a minimum amount of damage. Soft-nose bullets penetrate tissue but mushroom out when they hit bone; hollow points mushroom even more easily, causing tremendous damage at point of impact and maximizing the chances of a kill. Soft-nose and hollow-point ammunition are designed for game hunting, while full-jacketed bullets are used by the military. This is not pure humanitarianism on the part of the armed services, however—killing a man takes him out of action, but wounding him removes both him and the people needed to take care of him.

Some misguided people will file down or file a cross shape in the tip of a full-jacketed bullet to expose the lead beneath, thus creating what is known as a "dum dum" cartridge. When fired, this altered bullet will have the impact of a soft-nose or worse, and will do terrible damage to any living thing that it hits. This practice, however, is dangerous both to the shooter and the target. Since the dum dum's lead core is exposed at both ends, it is possible for the core to be pushed through the bullet's jacket and carry on to the target, leaving the jacket wedged tightly in the gun's barrel. With the next shot fired, the gun will quite possibly blow up in the shooter's face.

DEATH ON THE *IOWA*

Problems in ballistics are often complex, and their solutions are always vital to the determination of a pending case. Yet no case has had a ballistics investigation larger in scope and importance than that of the tragedy that occurred on the battleship U.S.S. *Iowa* on April 19, 1989.

During a routine gunnery training exercise, an explosion in the breech of the middle weapon of the three sixteen-inch guns in *Iowa*'s Gun Turret Number 2 resulted in the almost immediate deaths of forty-seven seamen. The *Iowa*'s sixteen-inch guns are fearsome weapons, capable of hurling a 2,700-pound projectile—equal to the weight of a small car—a distance of twenty-four miles and hitting a target the size of a bus. Depending on the desired target range, it takes five, six, or seven 93.4-pound bags of nitrocellulose gunpowder to toss the gun's massive bullet to its destination. On April 19, 1989, a five-bag load totalling more than 460 pounds of gunpowder exploded inside the armored turret, instantly killing everyone in the turret's central gun room and reaching down a total of five floors below for additional victims. However, thanks to a complicated series of safeguards designed to prevent enemy gunfire from penetrating to the ship's powder room, a second massive explosion—one that would probably have destroyed the ship—was prevented.

The navy needed to know the cause of the explosion, and it needed to know quickly: Three other World War II–era battleships had been recently recommissioned (as there have been no battleships built since that war), and if there was a fatal flaw in the loading system, mechanism, or the aging powder, it had to be found and fixed as soon as possible. All of the big guns were silenced while the investigation continued.

Evidence as to causes was hard to come by. The blast itself did a good job of destroying everything inside the turret, and the subsequent fire—and the water and foam poured on it by the firefighters—just about completed the job.

The navy spent four months writing a report, in which they gave their equipment a clean bill of health and put the blame on the sabotage tactics of one victim, twenty-four-year-old petty officer Clayton Hartwig, who had been gun captain of Turret Number 2 at the time of the explosion. Hartwig, the navy report said, was despondent over the breaking off of a homosexual relationship with Gunnar's Mate 3/c Kendall L. Truitt, a crewmate who had recently been married. As evidence the report cited the $50,000 double-indemnity life insurance policy carried by Hartwig with Truitt as the beneficiary and Hartwig's possession of a book called *Getting Even: The Complete Book of Dirty Tricks*. To support this theory the navy report cited their psychological profile of Hartwig and that the investigation had uncovered chemical traces amid the wreckage of what was claimed to have been an "ignition device." For a while the navy considered blaming Truitt, but could find no plausible way for him to have planted the sabotage device; he was working in the bottom tier of the turret when it blew up, a position he would assuredly have avoided if he knew the explosion was going to occur.

This explanation, although it conveniently allowed the remaining big guns to commence firing, satisfied no one but the naval brass. Hartwig's family was incensed. Truitt denied being a homosexual, and the navy admitted that it had no evidence of homosexual behavior on the part of either him or Hartwig. And the report glossed over substantial safety problems that had been found in the ship's gun handling.

So what did happen? Unsatisfied with the official navy report, the Senate Armed Services Committee was determined to find out and in November 1989 asked Sandia National Laboratories to investigate.

Sandia has been conducting weapons and explosives research since it was founded to help build atomic weapons and is probably one of the few places in the world capable of putting together an in-house team of the experts required for such an investigation. But the event was already a year old, and the chance of getting any new data seemed remote.

Sandia's first task was to examine the known sequence of events as well as the theory navy investigators had drawn from the facts they had.

The gun room for the central sixteen-inch gun of the *Iowa*'s Turret Number 2 is manned by four men: the gun captain, the primerman, the cradleman, and the rammerman. The loading sequence is supposed to go like this: The projectile, a 2,700-pound bullet the size of a man, is brought up to the gun room from below decks on a hydraulic hoist. Normally it would be a high-explosive projectile, but since this was a practice firing, it was filled with a dummy charge. The primerman inserts the primer, which resembles a .30-caliber blank, into the breech of the gun. Then the cradleman moves the projectile onto a cradle which feeds into the breech. At a signal from the gun captain, the rammerman pushes a lever which activates a rammer, giving the projectile a powerful and speedy push into the breech of the sixty-six-foot-long barrel.

The next step is the tricky one. The bags of gunpowder are brought up from a different below deck location by a second lift, called the powder hoist car. Once the projectile is seated in the barrel, the rammerman moves a lever opening the powder hoist door (which, as a safety measure, will not open unless the one at the bottom of the shaft is closed), and the bags of propellant are rolled onto the cradle. The rammerman then closes the powder hoist door, and the gun captain inserts between the first and second bags a thin lead foil packet designed to clean and lubricate the barrel when the gun is fired. At a signal from the gun captain, the rammerman then works the rammer lever to slowly—*slowly*—push the bags of gunpowder into the breech behind the projectile.

Then the rammer is extracted, the cradle is moved back, the gun captain and the primerman work three levers to close the breech, and the gun is ready to fire. A well-trained crew can complete this deadly ballet in half a minute, but anything up to a minute is considered adequate.

On the day of the accident, the left-gun crew reported it loaded in forty-four seconds, and the right crew loaded in sixty-one seconds. A few seconds later the rammer on the center gun called into the intercom: "I have a problem here, I'm not ready yet." And then, eighty-three seconds into the loading sequence, the center gun room exploded.

The navy's investigation decided that "probably" Hartwig, the gun captain, had placed an "incendiary device" between the first and second bags of powder at the same time he inserted the lead foil cleaning packet. The device they hypothesized was a plastic meal-ration bag filled with a mixture of

USS IOWA Turret Two
Just Before Explosion

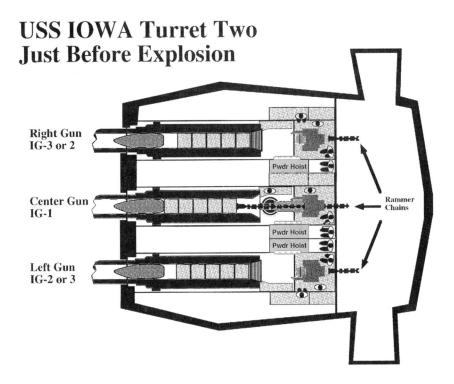

Right Gun IG-3 or 2

Center Gun IG-1

Left Gun IG-2 or 3

Pwdr Hoist

Pwdr Hoist

Pwdr Hoist

Rammer Chains

THIS IS A SCHEMATIC DIAGRAM OF 16" GUN TURRET TWO ON THE BATTLESHIP USS IOWA IMMEDIATELY BEFORE THE EXPLOSION. THE BREECHES OF THE LEFT AND RIGHT GUNS ARE CLOSED AND LOCKED, BUT THE BREECH OF THE CENTER GUN IS OPENED. THE RAMMER OF THE CENTER GUN IS EXTENDED WITH THE RAMMER HEAD AGAINST THE REARMOST POWDER BAG. NOTE THAT THE TRAINS OF POWDER BAGS IN THE LEFT AND RIGHT GUNS ARE IMMEDIATELY FORWARD OF THE BREECH DOOR. IN THE CENTER GUN THE TRAIN OF POWDER BAGS HAS BEEN RAMMED FORWARD UNTIL IT CONTACTS THE BASE OF THE 16" PROJECTILE. THE DOOR OF THE CENTER GUN DEPARTMENT POWDER HOIST IS OPENED, WHEREAS THE DOORS IN THE LEFT AND RIGHT GUNS ARE CLOSED, AS THEY SHOULD BE FOR FIRING.

steel wool, brake fluid, and calcium hypochlorite (an oxygen supplier). This combination might ignite under the pressure of the ramming and set off the whole powder charge. Hartwig, to make sure of this, could have ordered his rammer to overram, thus thrusting the powder bags further into the barrel and perhaps hard against the projectile. The navy based this hypothesis on foreign material that investigators found imbedded in the copper-nickel ring encircling the projectile.

When the projectile had been removed from where it had been lodged by the explosion—some four feet up the sixty-six-foot barrel—this copper-nickel ring had been carefully examined. The ring, which is made of a significantly softer alloy than that of both the projectile and the barrel, forms the seal between the projectile and the barrel and also squeezes into the spiral rifling in the barrel, thus imparting a stabilizing spin to the projectile. In the process, the ring is bent over, trapping particles from the explosion behind it between the ring and the projectile.

The navy investigators found particles of three suspicious substances lodged in this pocket under the ring: steel wool with embedded calcium and chlorine; polyethylene terephthalate (PET), a plastic of the sort used to make plastic bags; and glycol, a constituent of brake fluid. On this, and a questionable psychological profile of Hartwig, they based their conclusions.

The Sandia experts began by looking closely at a section of the copper ring, examining the residue on it with the aid of spectroscopes and scanning electron microscopes, and all the other tools of the modern chemical analyst. They also took samples from various locations in the other gun rooms on the *Iowa*, and from the battleships *New Jersey* and *Wisconsin*, for comparison.

The lab experts found steel fibers in several other turrets, along with traces of both calcium and chlorine. Rather than necessarily coming from a suicide device, they noted, these elements are abundant in ordinary sea water. Calcium was also an ingredient of a lubricant known as Break Free used frequently by the navy and that actually had been used to help loosen the

How Debris is Trapped in Cannelure and Forward Grooves by Motion Up the Barrel

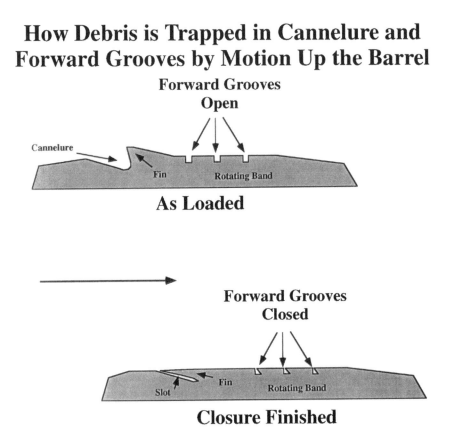

THE ROTATING BAND IS A STRIP OF COPPER-NICKEL ALLOY WHICH STRETCHES AROUND THE BASE OF THE 16" PROJECTILES. AS THE SHELL IS PUSHED INTO THE BARREL OF THE GUN THE FIN IS PUSHED DOWN ON THE CANNELURE TO FORM A GAS TIGHT SEAL BETWEEN THE PROJECTILE AND THE GUN BARREL. THE FORWARD GROOVES ALSO CLOSE AS THE SHELL IS PUSHED INTO THE BARREL BY THE GAS GENERATED FROM THE IGNITED POWDER. THE SCIENTISTS AT SANDIA ANALYZED THE PARTICLES TRAPPED IN THE CANNELURE AND THE FOWARD GROOVES, AND REACHED A DIFFERENT CONCLUSION FROM THAT OF THE NAVY INVESTIGATORS.

Iron Fibers Were Found In The Cannelure And The Forward Grooves

Forward Grooves

IG-2

Cannelure
IG-1

Iron
Fiber

Iron
Fiber

IG-1

DEBRIS IN THE CANNELURE OF THE ROTATING BAND OF THE CENTER GUN PROJECTILE (IG-1) INCLUDED TINY IRON FIBERS, WHICH THE NAVY INVESTIGATORS ATTRIBUTED TO STEEL WOOL FROM A CHEMICALLY IGNITED INCENDIARY DEVICE. SANDIA SCIENTISTS FOUND IDENTICAL IRON FIBERS IN THE FORWARD GROOVES OF PROJECTILES FROM THE UNINVOLVED GUNS (IG-2, UPPER RIGHT PHOTO). THIS BROUGHT INTO QUESTION THE NAVY'S CONCLUSIONS.

projectile stuck forty-four inches up the gun barrel. The investigators also found PET traces in several of the other gun rooms, noting that the substance is a common plastic used in, among many other things, buttons and ball-point pen barrels.

Then there was the glycol. Three different types of glycol had been identified. The Sandia investigators found that one of them was a constituent of Break Free; one turned out not to be a glycol at all, but rather a phenol, and was also found in Break Free; and the third glycol was ubiquitous—its presence could not be used to prove anything.

Having demolished the navy's theory of what caused the explosion, Sandia was now faced with the task of coming up with a theory of its own and then proving it.

Before deciding on the sabotage theory, the navy had worked hard to see if the explosion could have been accidental. They had tried blowing up the bags of powder by various sorts of impact, simulating as closely as they could the actual conditions within the gun room, but the bags of powder stubbornly refused to ignite. This was a relief to the navy, since the powder in use for the big guns, a nitrocellulose mixture called Navy Cool, dated back to the Korean War and was known to be unstable after long periods of time. For use in these powder bags, the Korea-era Navy Cool had been remixed and regrained into uniform two-inch long segments resembling sticks of green classroom chalk before roughly 1,800 of them were packed into each silk bag. The navy was not displeased when its tests showed that the Navy Cool had not been set off by accident.

But Karl Schuler, head of the Sandia team, was not so sure. The navy had noted one anomalous event in the center gun room: a twenty-one-inch overram. That is, the rammer had pushed the gunpowder bags twenty-one inches too far into the barrel. But this should not have caused an explosion, since it would have put the bags next to, but not pushed up against, the projectile. This overram was established by the presence of deep gouges in the tray that cradled the powder bags as they were shoved into the breech. Schuler noted that the bronze tip of the rammer should not have left gouges in the harder metal of the tray, but that the steel chain behind the tip might have. This would have meant that there was actually a *twenty-four-inch* overram, which would have slammed the gunpowder bags up against the base of the projectile.

Schuler and his team also noted that the powder hoist had not been lowered at the time of the blast. Lowering it was standard operating procedure; but suppose the blast had occurred before the hoist operator had a chance to lower it? This would indicate that the rammer had not only gone in too far, but *much too fast*. Perhaps the rammerman, a trainee who had never handled live ammunition before, had made a mistake, and not only overrammed but at an unsafe speed. The hypothesis made sense, but only if such a mistake would actually set off the powder. The Sandia crew set out to test this.

Paul Cooper of Sandia's explosive studies team set up a test site at Kirtland Air Force Base outside of Albuquerque. The navy forwarded them twelve bags of Navy Cool propellant, packaged in the same manner as those used by the *Iowa*. Cooper and his fellow explosives teammates examined the bags and noticed one possible focus for their attention: The chalk-sized sticks of propellant were packed in eight layers of about 225 sticks each, with a few odd sticks put in a "trim layer" on top to bring the weight of each bag to exactly 93.4 pounds. That top layer consists of anywhere from fifteen to sixty-five pellets lying on their sides. The Sandia people wondered what would happen if the side-lying trim layer were smashed up hard against, say, the base of the projectile by a rapid overram.

The explosives team conducted 450 drop tests over the next several months and confirmed their suspicions. Pellets in the trim layer could crack and spark if they were smashed too hard. And the fewer pellets in any given trim layer, the more chance of it happening, as each pellet would be subjected to a greater force. Sandia notified the navy of its findings, and full-scale tests were arranged.

Late in May 1990, thirteen months after the explosion, scientists and technicians watched from a bunker as an 810-pound steel weight was dropped on silk bags of Navy Cool gunpowder. Seventeen times, nothing happened. Then Schuler rearranged the top layer of one of the bags into what he thought was a likely configuration of pellets. On the eighteenth drop, the powder went off, blowing apart the test rig. As Schuler told a reporter from *Popular Science* magazine, "There was a dead silence in the bunker, then someone uttered an expletive."

No one will ever know for sure what happened that April afternoon in the center gun room of Turret Number 2, but, as Roger Hagengruber, a Sandia vice president, put it, "We usually find that the simplest possible explanation consistent with the evidence is the most defensible. Sabotage was not the simplest explanation consistent with the evidence."

On the basis of the Sandia findings, the navy temporarily suspended firing the big guns and revised the standard loading procedures. After a long wait—and one of the most complex ballistics investigations in history—the family of petty officer Clayton Hartwig was vindicated.

The removal of bullets from a crime scene requires special handling and attention. Since a bullet usually does not just drop where it is found, but has been propelled with some force into the object in which it is embedded, an examination of the path it took in entering the object can reveal how far away and in what direction the gun was when it was fired. This can be useful both in reconstructing the crime and testing the reliability of the testimony of witnesses or suspects.

If a bullet is embedded, the technician cannot merely dig it out with a knife blade or awl. This will destroy both the individual stress markings on the bullet and the line of the entrance hole. A better procedure is to carefully remove the small section of wall containing the bullet and take it away to the lab for examination. The direction the bullet was fired from should be determined before the piece of wall is removed.

If the criminalist finds some shell casings at the crime scene she may be able to glean some useful information from them. Given that the criminal does not carry spent shells around in his pocket with a compulsive need to scatter them about at the scene of his crime, one useful conclusion is that the gun used was an automatic. As part of the process of chambering the next round to fire, the automatic pistol ejects the spent cartridge case. Bolt and lever-action rifles also eject the shell casing when

THE VARIETY OF DESIGN OF SHELL CASINGS AND
BULLETS IS VAST. HERE ARE A FEW EXAMPLES.

the weapon is rechambered. Confirmation of the type of firearm used can sometimes come from the shells themselves, as cartridges designed for the automatic are often of a slightly different shape than those for the revolver of the same caliber, particularly at the rim.

When the firing pin strikes the primer it punches an indentation; the appearance of this marking will remain constant from shot to shot and can be used to identify the specific gun a shell was fired from. The ejection mechanism may also leave an indentation on the side of the shell, and there may be characteristic scratches along the shell, possibly only visible under a microscope, caused by the gun mechanism. The technician collecting the spent cartridges must be careful not to do anything that might add to or obliterate these possibly characteristic scratches.

If a suspect in a case where a gun was used can be examined within six hours of the time the gun was fired, gunshot residue (GSR) evidence may be gathered from the suspected shooter's hands. The dermal nitrate test—which became famous in crime fiction as the "paraffin test," in which liquid wax is poured over the suspect's hands and then peeled off and tested for the presence of nitrates—is no longer used. Nitrates are present in both black and smokeless powder residue, but unfortunately they are also present in fertilizer, manure, and a variety of other common substances as well.

The tests used now to detect gunshot residue are known as neutron activation analysis (NAA), atomic absorption spectrophotometry (AA), and scanning electron microscopy/energy dispersive x-ray analysis (SEM/EDX). What these newer GSR procedures test for is a deposit of barium and antimony, two components of the primer charge used in nearly all ammunition. The deposit shows up most strongly in the webbed area between the thumb and forefinger. A series of cotton swabs dipped in a dilute nitric acid solution are rubbed over the hands of the suspect—separate swabs for the palms and backs of the hands, with an extra swab for the cartridge case if it has been found, and a test control swab.

These GSR tests are not absolute, only indicative. A negative result may mean that the suspect did not fire the weapon, but it may also mean that he was wearing rubber gloves, or held the gun in a plastic baggie, or that the weapon was so well made that no residue escaped. A positive result may mean that the suspect did fire the murder weapon, but it could also mean that he fired some other weapon, or that he merely held the weapon but did not fire it.

After a careful search the Gotham City forensic evidence team found an expended .32-caliber cartridge casing under a filing cabinet, where it had obviously rolled. It was bagged and an evidence card was filled out, noting where and by whom the cartridge was found. They located the slug fired from Daniels's gun in the wall across from the desk. It had made a neat, round hole in the plasterboard, passed through the hollow space, and actually embedded itself on the inside of the plasterboard facing the other wall. The two technicians used a length of string to trace the angle at which the bullet had entered the wall. This experiment yields only approximate results; it cannot show the exact spot the gun was held when it was fired. In this case it did indicate that Daniels was sitting behind his desk when he fired the shot. Since the powder burns on his chest indicated that his assailant must have been within three feet, the probability was that Daniels's murderer had been sitting in front of the desk.

After taking photographs and drawing rough maps with all distances marked, the technicians cut out the piece of wall containing the bullet, boxed it carefully, and took it and the bagged shell casing to the lab.

In the laboratory the technicians extracted the bullet from the wall and examined it under the microscope. Embedded in the tip were tiny strands of a gray wool fabric, possibly from a jacket—giving an indication of what the bullet had passed through on its way to the wall. If a jacket were found with a bullet hole in it, and its fabric matched the fibers found on the bullet, this would be strong presumptive evidence that whoever had been wearing the jacket had been in the study at the time of the murder.

FIVE

THE FICKLE FINGER

FINDING THE PRINT

The crime scene investigators at the Daniels's house scoured the room, the surrounding area, and the corpse for fingerprints. They also took the prints of the defunct Mr. Daniels and his wife to eliminate them from the fingerprints they found on the scene. Before they took the corpse's prints they went over his hands with a series of swabs dipped in nitric acid to see if he had fired a gun recently, as we noted in the last chapter.

A partial print that did not come from either Mr. or Mrs. Daniels was found on the shell casing that had been retrieved from under the file cabinet. There was some detritus in the small wastebasket in the bathroom, including a bandage with the print of what was certainly a thumb impressed perfectly in blood. The criminalists now had two suspicious single prints to work with. Often a single print can be used to identify someone from the fingerprint files, if the criminal has been bad enough or notorious enough for the department to keep a single-print breakdown on him in addition to the usual ten-print classification. This, unfortunately, was not one of those times. However, if a suspect was found, the single prints would be enough to establish him as the person who had loaded the murder weapon or who had left the bloody thumbprint in the bathroom—or both.

The greatest advance in thief-taking since the invention of the police whistle was certainly the discovery of fingerprints as an immutable personal signature. The fingerprints you were born with can be recognized as yours a hundred years later. They will have changed in size and dimension, but in both the gross and fine detail there will have been little change, except for possible scarring and external deformation. And a scar does not change the print, it merely obscures that part of the print it lies over. This simple truth, combined with the fact that when a person touches something he often leaves behind a print of his finger—formed of sweat, body oil, grease, dust, blood, or some other material—makes fingerprint analysis possible. Inadvertently left fingerprints are of three types: visible, plastic, and latent.

Visible prints are the sort that small children leave on refrigerator doors when retrieving the milk after eating peanut-butter-and-jelly sandwiches. The transmitting medium may be grease, dirt, ink, paint, blood—or peanut butter and jelly.

Plastic prints are indentations left in objects soft or pliable enough to take and hold an impression, such as warm wax, soft soap, butter, putty, or drying paint.

Latent prints are left by perspiration or grease and tend to be invisible, although light striking a glossy surface at just the right angle might make such a print stand out enough to be seen.

The fingerprint technician's job is to locate fingerprints left at a crime scene, develop the latent prints, and preserve and prepare all useful prints for observation and identification. He will begin by taking the fingerprints of everyone who has a legitimate reason to be at the scene, including any police officers present, to use for elimination purposes, since people have a habit of touching things even when they know they're not supposed to. Then he will search for latent prints, "lift" the prints he finds onto index cards if possible, and mark each card with the time and location the print was lifted.

The earliest method for finding and developing latent prints involved the use of a finely divided powder like carbon-black, which was spread over the area to be examined with a soft brush or an insufflator (much like a perfume atomizer). If there was a latent print present, the powder adhered to it, and the excess could be blown away. Then the print could be "lifted" using transparent tape and placed on the index card.

Fingerprints can be left on almost anything and these days can be lifted or otherwise secured from just about any surface. The amount of time a latent print can last varies from moments to centuries. On a nonporous surface in cold, dry weather, the life of a latent print will probably be brief. In damp weather on porous surfaces it may exist for weeks. On newsprint or other non-glossy papers, it may survive for the life of the paper—latent prints have been recovered from ancient Egyptian papyri.

Although other methods of developing latent prints have been found that are superior in some circumstances, dusting with a fine powder is still used today. The choice of powder to be used depends mainly on the material and color of the object to be examined. The powder must stick to the fingerprint moisture or oil but not to the background, and it must show up well in contrast to the background color. Usually a black powder is used on light colored surfaces and a gray powder on dark or black surfaces, but selecting the best powder for a specific surface from the many powders available is, even today, more of an art than a science.

The first fingerprint powders were made of finely divided white, gray, and red lead. Although these powders were highly effective, unfortunately they were also highly toxic, and thus the use of lead-based powders has all but ceased. A very good choice when a black powder is required today is the fine carbon powder used to refill photocopy machines.

Each print lifted must be immediately identified. If it is put onto a lift card—often a blank three-by-five-inch file card—it is put as close to one edge as possible, with the other half of the card containing a description of where the print was lifted from, sometimes with a little sketch of the room and an X to mark the spot. The technician lifting the print and his or her partner will initial each card, ideally as it is created and certainly before they leave the room, and will include the date and time.

IDENTIFYING THE PRINT

The fingerprints of Mrs. Daniels and William Batson, her dining partner, were sent by computer to the central fingerprint archive in the state capital, as well as to the FBI National Crime Information Center (NCIC). It was a precaution rather than a suspicion, and as the investigators had assumed, neither set of prints matched any of those on either criminal register.

There was naturally the strong possibility that one of Daniels's more criminous clients had something to do with the crime. The morning after the murder the two homicide detectives appeared in the offices of the defunct attorney to obtain a list of his clients. At first Daniels's faithful secretary, Herbert Hackenbush, was hesitant to give out the list of names. But when the detectives pointed out that it was a matter of court record, and all he was doing was saving them time—and perhaps helping to catch his boss's murderer—Hackenbush decided to cooperate.

The detectives passed the list of names on to the records division, who began to pull the files and fingerprint cards of all who had criminal records. Judging by Daniels's legal practice, that would be most of them.

In the United States the practice of fingerprinting and keeping fingerprint files began in the major penitentiaries. Sing Sing started in March 1903, and the other New York State prisons took it up shortly after. The federal penitentiary in Leavenworth, Kansas, switched from anthropometry—the system devised by French criminologist Alphonse Bertillon of measuring body parts—to fingerprinting toward the end of 1904.

Leavenworth was convinced of the need to convert because of an incident that had happened the year before. In 1903 a black prisoner named Will West was being measured for the Bertillon record then being used when warden R. W. McClaughty asked why a second file was being created for the prisoner. West protested that he had never been at Leavenworth, or any other prison, before. The warden pulled the old record of William West, convict number 2626, from the files, and confirmed that it corresponded to the prisoner's Bertillon measurements and that the photograph looked just like him. When Will West persisted in his denials the warden checked further and found that the William West of record 2626 was still a prisoner. The two men shared variants of the same name, looked the same down to the smallest detail, and their Bertillon measurements were practically identical. McClaughty had the prints of their left index fingers taken and compared, and was relieved to discover that, at least in that indicator, the two Wests were entirely different.

The fingerprint classification system used the characteristics of all ten prints and was most useful for identifying felons who had already been apprehended; the matching of single prints found at the scene of a crime was still a time-consuming task, almost impossible in a large database if there were no clue to the possible identity of the criminal. But if other evidence, such as eyewitness identification or the modus operandi file (a list of habitual criminals and their usual and oft repeated method of repeating their favorite crimes), could narrow down the search, then single-print identification could be done in a reasonable length of time and serve to positively identify the suspected felon.

A SHORT HISTORY OF FINGERPRINTS

In China the T'ang Dynasty bureaucracy (618–907) required the husband's thumbprint on the official documents for a divorce action. Eighth-century Japan had a similar law, presumably borrowed from China. Fingerprint contemplation stood there for a thousand years.

In 1684 Nehemiah Grew, a British doctor and a fellow of the College of Physicians and Surgeons of the Royal Society, published a lecture which discussed the ridge patterns on fingertips. In 1686 an Italian doctor named Marcello Malpighi published *De Externo Tactus Organo* (Concerning the External Organs of Feeling), in which he described the ridged pattern of the skin of the fingers and palm. However, neither of these gentlemen suggested that anything useful could be done with the information. It was another two hundred years before anyone attempted to classify fingerprints by type when, in 1823, Johannes Evangelist Purkinje divided fingerprints into nine groupings in a thesis for his Doctor of Medicine degree at the University of Breslau.

In 1858, William James Herschel, then employed by the East India Company, drew up a contract for road-building materials with a Bengali supplier named Rajyadhar Konai. In order to impress Konai with the seriousness of the contract, Herschel had him place his hand print—fingers and palm—on the back of the document. Herschel remembered this two years later when, now a magistrate at Nuddea, near Calcutta, he was charged with seeing that many natives received their government pensions. As most of the natives could neither read nor write and thus were unable to sign anything, the possibilities for fraud were endless. Herschel realized that fingerprints could serve as a positive means of identification. He began placing the pensioner's thumbprint on the receipt, and the number of fraudulent claims dropped dramatically.

For the next two decades Herschel continued his study of fingerprints, becoming convinced that the prints did not change with age and that no two were alike. In 1877 he wrote a letter to the inspector general of the prison system of Bengal outlining his researches with fingerprints. "I have taken thousands [of fingerprints] now in the course of the last twenty years, and I am prepared to answer for the identity of every person whose sign-manual I can now produce if I am confronted with him," he wrote.

The inspector general refused to give Herschel permission to try his system, even on a small scale in a local prison. Disillusioned and in poor health, Herschel returned to England in 1879.

While Herschel had been experimenting in India, Dr. Henry Faulds, a Scot who was serving as a resident at the Tsukiji Hospital in Tokyo, Japan, became fascinated with fingerprints when he noted the finger marks of the potter on specimens of prehistoric Japanese pottery. He began a systematic study of fingerprints, determining that each of the prints he collected was unique and that an individual's prints did not change over the course of his lifetime. Faulds also found that the best medium for transferring the prints was a thin film of printer's ink, on which the finger was rolled before being pressed and rolled on the fingerprint card, a method still in general use. In 1879 he was able to use his newly developing science to aid the local police catch a burglar, thus becoming the first person to solve a crime by fingerprint evidence.

A year later, on October 28, 1880, a letter from Faulds published in the British journal *Nature* outlined his discoveries and his proposal for establishing a scientific method of identification using fingerprints. He also discussed his own experience in using them to solve crimes, saying in part, "When bloody fingermarks or impressions on clay, glass, etc., exist, they may lead to the scientific identification of criminals." The next issue of *Nature* printed a reply from Herschel, who related his experiences in India. This began a feud between the two men over who could claim priority in the use of fingerprints for identification.

In 1882 in the New Mexico Territory of the United States, Gilbert Thompson, a government geologist, began using his own thumbprint on requisitions to prevent forgery. A year later Mark Twain published *Life on the Mississippi*, in which he describes the solving of a crime by the use of fingerprints. Twain's fascination with fingerprints continued, and ten years later a major plot point in his book *Pudd'n-head Wilson*, published in 1894, revolved around a courtroom identification based on fingerprint evidence.

In 1886 Faulds, back in Britain, offered to set up a fingerprint bureau for Scotland Yard at his own expense. The offer was rejected. Neither Herschel nor Faulds had developed a method of classifying fingerprints for later retrieval, and without a reliable classification system the value of fingerprints for identification was extremely limited.

In 1886 the noted British scientist Sir Francis Galton became interested in dactyloscopy, as the study of fingerprints had become known. Herschel kindly lent Galton his collection of fingerprint cards, and Galton spent the next three years establishing that fingerprints remained unchanged through a person's life and that it was at least theoretically possible to work out a method of classifying them. Using an extremely conservative estimate of the amount of variability in a given fingerprint, Galton calculated the probability of two sets of prints matching to be one in sixty-four million.

Galton put the results of his research into a book, *Finger Prints*, published in 1892. He had developed a tentative approach to the problem of indexing fingerprints based upon whether the pattern of each individual print was an arch, a loop, or a whorl. In 1893 the British Home Office established a committee headed by Charles Edward Troup (therefore known as the Troup Committee) to recommend a criminal identification system to be used by Scotland Yard. The Troupers consulted with Galton and were very impressed with the potential of fingerprint identification, as demonstrated by him in his laboratory. But Galton, the true scientist, explained to them that the system he had devised for categorizing and sorting the fingerprints was too complex and unwieldy for use outside of the laboratory, and it would be some years before a reliable system could be perfected.

The Troup Committee therefore recommended that the anthropometric system of Bertillon be adopted by Scotland Yard, but that it be supplemented by fingerprinting. Therefore a body of fingerprints would be available for comparison when the method to do so had been perfected. This suggestion was approved by Scotland Yard.

In 1894 the seventy-two-year-old Galton passed on the torch of dactyloscopy to Edward Henry, who carried it to success. Henry, who had read Galton's book *Finger Prints* in India where he had served as inspector general of the Bengal police, took a trip to England to meet Galton and discuss with him the future of fingerprint identification. Galton, with his usual generosity, talked to Henry for hours, explaining the problems he had solved as well as those remaining. Galton loaded Henry down with as many fingerprint cards and pages of notes and examples as the man could carry and sent him on his way.

For the next two years back in India, Henry worked on the problem, eventually settling on five basic patterns for fingerprints: arches, tented arches, radial loops (slanting toward the thumb), ulnar loops (slanting away from the thumb), and whorls. These he designated by the letters A, T, R, U, and W. He broke these designations down further by showing how a straight line could be drawn connecting two specific locations on a print, and the number of ridges cut by that line counted. These letters and numbers would produce a specific code for any fingerprint card holding all ten fingerprints, and any two investigators categorizing the same fingerprint card would come up with the same code.

The system was complex and required intensive effort to master, but it worked. Once it was in use no felon could hope to hide his previous record—or the existence of outstanding arrest warrants—from the police.

In July 1897, after a one-year trial, the Indian government officially replaced anthropometry with dactyloscopy in their criminal records system. In 1901 Henry was called back to London to head Scotland Yard's Criminal Investigation Division (CID), with the rank of assistant commissioner of police. He oversaw the adoption of his own system of fingerprinting as the sole means of criminal identification. It quickly proved its usefulness by turning the identification of criminals from a time-consuming task fraught with the possibility of error into a routine process as close to infallible as anything yet devised: If two fingerprint cards held matching prints, then they had been made by the same person—no question about it.

While Henry was perfecting his system, an Argentine detective named Juan Vucetich was independently developing a fingerprint system of his own. In 1891 he had set up an office of anthropometry for the Identification Bureau of the Central Police Department in La Plata. After working with anthropometry he became aware of its shortcomings and began to look for a better system. Vucetich read an article on Galton's research into fingerprint classification in the May 1891 issue of a French science magazine, and worked out his own system, devising four primary categories of fingerprints.

In 1892, while Vucetich was developing his system, a woman named Francesca Rojas, who lived in Moecochea, in the province of Buenos Aires, was found collapsed in her house having suffered serious stab wounds in the neck. Her two sons were lying dead, both with their throats cut. Rojas accused an ex-lover who lived nearby of committing the crimes. The police, at the request of their superiors in La Plata, cut a blood-stained section of wood out of the doorjamb and forwarded it to the Identification Bureau, where a fingerprint was found in the blood stain. It proved to be that of Rojas herself. She confessed to the crime and went to prison.

Despite this success Vucetich was forced to finance the development of fingerprint classification from his own meager salary for years. The authorities refused to consider switching from anthropometry—even when Vucetich identified twenty-three criminals in one day by their fingerprints alone after all had successfully fooled the Bertillon system. Finally, under a new police chief, the Vucetich system of classification was adopted by Argentina in 1894, and in 1896 anthropometry was officially dropped. In 1904 Vucetich explained his system in his book *Dactyloscopia Comparada*; in 1907 the French Académie des Sciences judged it the best of all they examined, and by 1912 it was in use in all the countries of South America.

Great Britain and most of Europe adopted the Galton-Henry system, with the exception of France, Belgium, and Egypt, who used an amalgam of the two systems. France also held on to anthropometry for the first half of the twentieth century.

For a while courts were cautious about accepting fingerprint evidence that was not corroborated by other evidence or testimony, but as the novelty of the technique wore off, fingerprints were seen as more reliable than eyewitness testimony.

One of the major advantages of fingerprint identification is the ease of record taking. Other unique features of human physiognomy have been suggested as possible bases for identification systems: the pattern of the retina, the pores of the tongue, the shape of the ear, brain waves, voice prints, and even nose prints. Forensic dentistry has proved invaluable in identifying corpses when fingerprints have been unavailable or impossible to take. DNA typing is now possible when a suspect has left blood, sera, or bits of flesh at the scene of the crime. But fingerprints still provide the most practical and most certain means of identification.

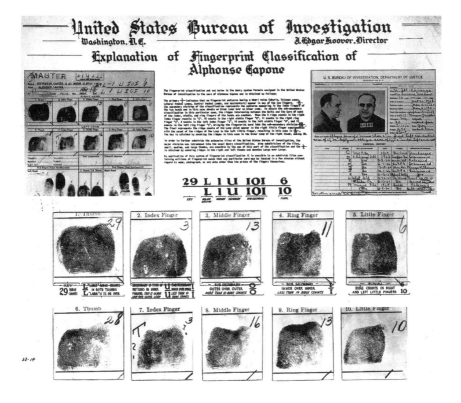

FBI IDENTIFICATION FINGERPRINT CARD FROM THE
1930s.

In 1924, the United States Congress authorized the Bureau of Investigation of the Justice Department (now the Federal Bureau of Investigation) to create and maintain the Identification Division. Fingerprint files of federal prisoners maintained at Leavenworth, Kansas, and a large collection that was being kept by the International Association for Chiefs of Police were combined, and the Identification Division began its existence with a collection of 810,188 prints. The collection grew rapidly. Eleven years later, on May 24, 1935, the Identification Division filed its 5 millionth card. The Identification Division's 10 millionth card, received on January 31, 1946, was that of actress Margaret O'Brien, taken while the then 9-year-old child star was taking a tour of FBI headquarters in Washington, D.C. As of February 1, 1991, the FBI had a total of 193,137,999 in its files, of which 107,058,738 were in the criminal division. The method devised for taking fingerprints by the early fingerprinters is pretty much the one still in use today. Printer's ink is spread evenly with a rubber roller on a glass plate, and then the person to be fingerprinted has his fingers rolled one at a time on the plate and then onto a fingerprint card, which is usually in some sort of card holder. After the individual fingerprints are taken each hand is inked as a whole and pressed onto the card. The reason the full handprint, called a flat print, is taken is to have a means of checking that each individual rolled print is indeed from the finger indicated by its position on the card.

Printer's ink or some similar ink is used because it dries quickly and because when rolled onto the finger it goes only onto the ridges and not into the creases, thus making a clear impression. Stamp pad inks, which have been used when nothing better is available, tend to give blurred impressions. Some fingerprint departments are now using fluids that leave the fingers clean and develop on the card, but these tend to be expensive and more difficult to use. Most departments—understaffed, undertrained, and underfinanced, or just too traditionalist to change—still use printer's ink.

The standard fingerprint record card, in use over most of the world, is an eight-inch square of medium-weight cardboard. The basic form still in use was devised in 1908 by P. A. Flak, a fingerprint expert working for the Library Bureau Company of Chicago, who designed it to be easy to file and retrieve. The actual information requested on the top of the card will vary from place to place and according to whether the form is a criminal identification card, a military record, or a civilian request, say for a job application. In any case, whatever the category or the recording agency, if the print is taken in the United States a copy will probably be sent to the F.B.I. to be put in the appropriate national registry.

The classification of fingerprint cards by the Galton-Henry Method (or as it's more commonly known, the Henry System) requires knowledge and training, and is neither self-evident nor simple. As Peter Laurie says in his book *Scotland Yard*, "To the layman, Henry's system appears to be one of the most obscure inventions of the human mind." But any two people properly trained in the system will come up with the same classification for the same fingerprint card.

The basics of the system are easy to understand. What makes them seem forbidding is their arcane logic and their resemblance to mathematics. Henry and his followers certainly had reasons for developing the system as they did. Perhaps it was a desire to keep the uninitiated from easily comprehending the secrets of dactyloscopy.

The pattern for any fingerprint can be put into one of four basic groups: arches, loops, whorls, or composites/accidentals. These patterns are formed by the ridges of the fingerprint, the raised lines that actually leave the inked impression on the paper or the unintentional impressions on objects in the environment. Fingers heavily scarred by injuries are merely classified as scars.

Arches are formed by ridges running from one side of the print to the other, curving upward in the middle. Usually the ridges above are more strongly curved than the ones below. Tented arches have a sort of spike like a tent pole going up the middle, with the arch curving over the top of the pole. The arch pattern makes up about 5 percent of all fingerprints.

Loops are curved more strongly than arches, and the ends of the loop enter and exit the print on the same side of the finger. Radial loops slant toward the thumb (or toward the radius bone of the forearm, which is the one on the thumb side), while Ulnar loops slant away from the thumb (or toward the ulna bone in the forearm, which is behind the radius).

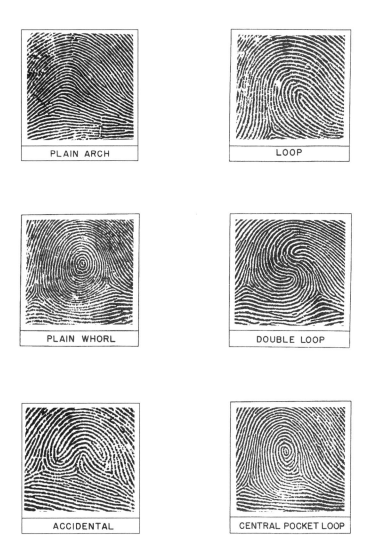

PLAIN ARCH

LOOP

PLAIN WHORL

DOUBLE LOOP

ACCIDENTAL

CENTRAL POCKET LOOP

FBI EXAMPLES OF BASIC FINGERPRINT TYPES.

When a single print is being evaluated, the investigator has no way to tell for sure whether a loop pattern is radial or ulnar unless it is known which hand the print is from. (The presumption would be that it is ulnar, since ulnar loops predominate.) Loops make up about 60 percent of all fingerprints.

Whorls form a complete oval, usually in an interconnected spiral pattern around a central point. They make up about 30 percent of all fingerprints.

Composites and accidentals, which make up the remaining 5 percent, are often grouped as subdivisions of whorls. Composites are formed of the intermixing of two or more of the basic patterns. There can be a loop that intersects a whorl, or a loop under an arch, or a twinned loop, or a small whorl within a larger whorl. Accidentals are those prints which are too irregular to be classified in any other group.

It takes practice in reading fingerprints to be able to classify them reliably, consistently, and reasonably quickly. There are many variants to be learned, and many close calls, but the great majority of fingerprints fall clearly into one of the established types. The classification of fingerprints is based on a formula that accounts for the type of print on each finger of both hands. In the Henry System and its modern variants, fingerprint cards are classified three or four separate ways to allow for enough variation so that any given card will not have too many others duplicating its exact classification.

Primary classification involves invoking a formula based on the number and location of whorls among the prints. The fingers are numbered consecutively from the right thumb to the left little finger, and a numeric value is given to each whorl-patterned fingerprint, as follows:

RIGHT HAND

1/Thumb	2/Index	3/Middle	4/Ring	5/Little
16	16	8	8	4

LEFT HAND

6/Thumb	7/Index	8/Middle	9/Ring	10/Little
4	2	2	1	1

As you can see, a whorl pattern on the thumb of the right hand has a numeric value of 16; a whorl pattern on the middle finger of the left hand has a numeric value of 2. Arches, loops, or accidentals on any finger have numeric values of zero.

The primary classification is a fraction created by adding the value of every print that is a whorl. Even-numbered fingers are added for the numerator (the top number of the fraction), and odd-numbered fingers are added for the denominator (the bottom number). Because a finger-print card with ten whorl-less prints would be classified 0/0, and the early classifiers thought that looked odd, they determined to add the number 1 to both numerator and denominator in all cases. With the one added, the lowest primary classification is 1/1, and the highest is 32/32.

For example: a set of fingerprints is examined and found to have whorls on the right thumb, right ring finger, left index finger, and left little finger. The right thumb and left index finger are odd numbered fingers, with values of 16 and 2, giving 18 for the numerator. The right ring finger and left little finger are even numbered, with values of 8 and 1, for a total of 9 for the denominator. Adding 1 to both sides, we come up with a primary classification of 19/10 for this fingerprint card.

There are 1,024 distinct primary classifications, which is enough of a breakdown as long as the fingerprint collection to be searched is low—say under two hundred thousand. But as fingerprinting became more popular with law enforcement, and the number of print records in major files ran into the millions, a further breakdown was needed.

Secondary classification assigns letters to the basic patterns: A = arch, T = tented arch, R = radial loop, U = ulnar loop, and W = whorl. A fraction is formed with the right hand above the line and the left hand below. The letter for each index finger is capitalized, the other fingers are in lower case. If the thumb is a whorl or an ulnar loop, it is left blank. If the middle or ring fingers are whorls or ulnar loops, and the following finger (on the right) is an arch, a tented arch, or a radial loop, the letter is replaced by a dash. If two or more fingers past the index finger have the same pattern, the number of fingers and the letter are used in place of a stuttering of the letter. Thus two consecutive arches would be "2a" rather than "a a." For example, a representative classification might be:

Right Thumb = Arch
    Index Finger = Tented Arch
    Middle Finger = Whorl
    Ring Finger = Radial Loop
    Little Finger = Radial Loop

Left Thumb = Ulnar Loop
    Index Finger = Whorl
    Middle Finger = Radial Loop
    Ring Finger = Radial Loop
    Little Finger = Whorl

The basic fraction would be:

$$\frac{\text{aTwrr}}{\text{uWrrw}}$$

and it would be reduced to:

$$\frac{\text{aT} - 2\text{r}}{\text{W2rw}}$$

Sub-secondary classification goes one step further. Only the middle three fingers are used, leaving the thumb and little finger out. This classification considers whorls and loops only, and gets into what is known as ridge counting. To understand ridge counting, you must understand what a delta is. A delta is arbitrarily defined as the first break in the pattern outside the area of the basic loop, whorl, or whatever the pattern is. By choice it will be a forked ridge (called a *bifurcation*) with the fork opening toward the center or *core* of the pattern. If there is no handy fork, then the closest other break in the pattern will be designated the delta. It could be an abrupt ridge-ending, an island (where a ridge separates briefly and then comes back together), a ridge fragment, or a dot. There is almost always something. Page after page of examples exist in the fingerprint handbooks to show exactly where the delta or core should be located in fingerprints that differ from the norm, so any given print can certainly be categorized.

The method of ridge counting is different for loops and whorls. Whorls are differentiated into three types: inner, meeting and outer, which are designated by the letters I, M, and O. To determine which type a given whorl is, first the deltas are located. Whorls tend to have two deltas, one on the left and one on the right. The ridge line directly under the left delta is followed to its point closest to the right delta, a procedure called tracing the ridge. The ridge lines between the right delta and this closest point are then counted. If the whorl passes inside the delta and there are three or more ridge lines, it is an inner (I). If it passes outside the delta by three or more lines, it is an outer (O). If it meets the delta or is no more than two lines away on either side, then it is a meeting whorl (M).

Loops are easier to categorize. The closest delta is located and a line is drawn from the delta to the center of the pattern. The ridges intersected by the line are counted. Neither the core nor the delta are included in the count. A high count (over nine on index fingers, over ten on middle fingers, and over thirteen on ring fingers) is an O. A lesser count is an I.

The fraction form is used again, right hand above and left hand below. A sub-secondary classification might look like this:

$$\frac{IOM}{MOO}$$

Final classification is often needed by very large police departments having vast collections of prints. If the right little finger is a loop, its ridge count is placed at the end of the numerator of the sub-secondary classification. If it is not—but the left little finger is—then its ridge count is placed at the end of the denominator. If neither is a loop, then there is no final classification. Some identification sections use either a loop or whorl for the final classification.

Many other divisions are possible, and some departments use further classifications, such as a ridge count on thumbs that are either loops or whorls.

The Vucetich System classification method, in use throughout most of South America, is quite different from the Henry System, although still based on recognition of arches, loops, whorls, accidentals, and composites. It uses a combination of letters and numbers to identify the finger patterns—letters for the thumb and numbers for the fingers. They are:

A or 1 for an arch.

I or 2 for a loop pointing to the left (on either hand, ulnar and radial designations are not used)

E or 3 for a loop pointing to the right.

V or 4 for all whorls, composites, and accidentals.

Thus the fingerprint pattern described above in Henry as:

$$\frac{aT - 2r}{W2rw}$$

would, in Vucetich, become:

$$\frac{A1433}{I4224}$$

The numbering system continues for further breakdown of the prints. People familiar with both systems say that the Vucetich system is easier to learn.

More than a hundred fingerprint systems have been used throughout the world over the past century, and more than fifty are still in use today. Most are modifications of the Henry or the Vucetich systems, although computerized systems are gradually forcing the older ones out. Here are some of the more important or interesting systems:

The Bertillon System is Bertillon's modification of the Vucetich System.

The Collins Single Fingerprint System, developed by Scotland Yard Superintendent Charles Collins was devised as a method of sending a Henry ten-print description plus a more detailed description of a single print over a teletype.

The Oloriz System, basically the Vucetich System with a hint of Henry, came into use in Madrid in 1910. In addition to the central police file, registration books, containing descriptions and fingerprint classifications of all known criminals and suspects in Madrid, were carried by the Madrid police.

The Pottecher System, introduced in Indochina in 1902, has a slight resemblance to the Vucetich System and uses a measuring instrument called the Gabarit.

The Roscher System was developed by Roscher of the Hamburg Police. A combination of the Henry and Vucetich systems, it uses the Henry method of pattern division (A, R, U, and W) as well as ridge counting. It numbers the fingers and uses the same numbers for the thumbs, where Vucetich uses letters. It also places the left hand above the right in the inevitable fingerprint fraction, the opposite of most other systems.

The Steegers System, introduced in Cuba by Juan Steegers, was essentially the Henry system with the names translated into Spanish, though it added one interesting feature. The fingerprints were not taken on cardboard card stock, but rather on transparent photographic paper, which greatly simplified the process of reproducing the prints.

The identification of single fingerprints, which is essential to the solving of crimes since perpetrators are rarely considerate enough to leave latent prints of all ten fingers at the crime scene, is an extremely difficult problem. Not only are there ten times as many single prints as there are sets of prints, but very often it is impossible to tell just which finger left the print.

One of the first successful systems for single-print classification, known as *the Battley System,* was devised by Chief Inspector Harry Battley while he was in charge of the Fingerprint Bureau at Scotland Yard. It uses a special magnifying glass with a fixed focus, resembling the device philatelists use to examine postage stamps. At the base, sitting directly over the fingerprint to be examined, is a plain glass square with seven circles inscribed like a bullseye around a central dot. The inner circle has a radius of 3 millimeters, and each successive circle has a radius 2 mm wider. The circles are lettered consecutively, from the inside out, from **A** to **G**, and whatever lies outside the widest scribe is labelled **H**.

First, the print to be categorized is labelled according to an extended version of the Henry labels: arch, exceptional arch (radial or ulnar), tented arch, loop (radial or ulnar), whorl, central pocket loop, twinned loop, lateral pocket loop (radial or ulnar), accidental, scar or questioned pattern. The central dot of the Battley glass is placed in a specified place for each pattern, and the location by lettered circle of the first prominent feature; delta in the case of a loop, recurving ridge in the case of an arch, is noted. To this is added a number from 1 to 5 indicating what the core type is and the letter I, M or O if it is an inner, meeting, or outer design. There are also several further subdivisions possible.

Although the Battley system does cluster prints of similar appearance together, making it easier to search for a single print if needed, it is a labor-intensive system which, because of the inordinate amount of time necessary to search the files for a match, can only be used in cases of serious crime.

Today, after a century of Galton-Henry and Vucetich and their imitators, adapters, combiners, improvers, simplifiers, and translators, the field of dactyloscopy is undergoing a dramatic change. The computer has brought a degree of speed and accuracy to fingerprint finding that could never have been hoped for before. The FBI began testing computers in its Identification Division in 1972, and by 1980 began computerizing the Criminal Fingerprint File. On June 5, 1989, computer processing of fingerprint cards went on line and immediately cut the response time on the average request from two weeks to one day.

The computer opens wide a gateway to the past that would without it remain effectively closed. In 1990 the Los Angeles Police Department put a new computer on line that tied into the state's Automated Fingerprint Identification System (AFIS). In testing the fingerprint computer, the Latent Print Department entered fingerprints obtained at the scene of about fifty unsolved homicide cases dating from the 1960s. (There would have been no point in trying to match prints from other crimes, since the statute of limitations would have run out on anything but murder.)

One of the cases entered was that of a woman who had been murdered nearly thirty years before. On the morning of Friday, October 4, 1963, Thora Marie Rose, a forty-three-year-old divorcee who worked as a waitress at King's Drug Store in West Los Angeles, was found viciously beaten and strangled to death in the bedroom of her small apartment at 1315 North Detroit Street. She had spent the evening before dancing at the Continental Hotel in Hollywood, returning to her apartment around midnight or one in the morning. Sometime between then and dawn someone had removed three of the glass louvers from a window at the rear of her apartment and crawled inside. Once there he savagely beat Rose with what police believe was a claw hammer and then wrapped a silk stocking around her neck to strangle her. She was not sexually assaulted and no valuables seem to have been taken, but police detectives who worked on the case described it as one of the bloodiest assaults they had ever seen.

Los Angeles policeman Arnold Sauro, the fingerprint expert who examined the crime scene, lifted thirty-five prints from the apartment, including some from the window louvers, the kitchen sink, and the bedroom walls. When he matched them up he found that he had all five fingers from the killer's right hand and four from his left hand. With an almost full set of prints like that, it should have been a matter of routine to match them from the files.

But to everyone's surprise the prints didn't match the prints of anyone who was in the LAPD files or the state's files in Sacramento. There were no other useful clues to go on, and there the case lay moribund for twenty-seven years.

The computer, hunting through the millions of prints on line to compare them with those found on the wall of Thora Marie Rose's apartment all those years before, did in a matter of hours what would take a team of human analysts a number of years. It found a match—the prints of Vernon Robinson, a resident of Minneapolis, Minnesota.

At the time of Thora Marie Rose's murder, Robinson, who grew up in Los Angeles, had been an eighteen-year-old recruit attending the navy basic training center in San Diego. After getting out of the navy he had been in trouble with the law several times on drug- and alcohol-related charges, and spent three years in San Quentin. But then he turned his life around, joined Alcoholics Anonymous, and held down a series of steady jobs, each new one an improvement on the last. At the time of the print match-up, he was a $70,000-a-year executive at a building-maintenance firm in Minneapolis.

When confronted with the evidence, Robinson denied any knowledge of the murder, claiming that he was in training at the San Diego base at the time. Unfortunately the navy's records showed that he had completed training the week prior. Robinson was extradited to Los Angeles in 1992 and put on trial for the 1963 murder of Thora Marie Rose. Steven Meagher, an FBI fingerprint expert, compared the latent prints found at the crime scene with new prints taken from Robinson and found them to be an exact match, thus once again establishing that prints do not change appreciably over time.

In 1993 Vernon was convicted of a thirty-year-old murder and sentenced to life in prison.

NCIC III FPC

In 1983 the FBI opened the National Crime Information Center (NCIC), a computerized information system designed to expedite the exchange of information between and among law enforcement agencies at all levels. As part of the system, the FBI set up the Interstate Identification Index (III), a sort of master file of felons, containing information on millions of people with criminal records gleaned from federal, state, and local files. Since different jurisdictions have slightly different ways of classifying fingerprints, the FBI has introduced a standard system, known as the NCIC Fingerprint Classification (FPC), by which this information will be uniformly transmitted.

The FPC works thus: the fingers are numbered as usual, from one to ten, with the right thumb being number 1, and the left thumb number 6. Each finger is allotted two characters. If the print is a plane arch, the NCIC FPC code is AA; if a tented arch, it is TT; if a radial loop, it is the ridge count plus 50 (i.e., if the ridge count is 14, the number entered is 64); if it is an ulnar loop, the number is the ridge count (with a preceding 0 if it is less than ten; if the count is seven ridges, the code is 07); if it is a plain whorl, the letter P is used, followed by a letter designating the tracing result (I for inner tracing; M for meeting tracing; and O for outer tracing); if a central pocket loop whorl, the letter C is followed by the tracing letter (I, M, or O); if a double loop whorl, the letter **d** followed by the tracing letter (if possible, the FBI suggests using the lower case **d**, as a handwritten capital D can be confused with an O); if an accidental whorl, the letter X followed by the tracing result letter (I, M, or O); a missing finger is designated XX; and a finger too badly scarred or mutilated to read the pattern is SR.

Thus the pattern that we described above in Henry:

$$\frac{aT - 2r}{W2rw}$$

would be described in FPC (with ridge counts and whorl tracings added) as:

AATTPI626409PO5860PM

The major advantage to the FPC system is that a straight-line number is easier to send over teletype, or for that matter telephone, than is a fraction, and reduces the possibility of error.

SIX

WHO WAS THAT
MASKED MAN?

> *If nature had only one fixed standard for the proportions of the various parts, then the faces of all men would resemble each other to such a degree that it would be impossible to distinguish one from another; but she has varied the five parts of the face in such a way that although she has made an almost universal standard as to their size, she has not observed it in the various conditions to such a degree as to prevent one from being clearly distinguished from another . . .*

— LEONARDO DA VINCI,
NOTEBOOKS

A man, or possibly two men, were seen entering the Daniels home shortly before Mr. Daniels was killed. Who were they? A pair of partial fingerprints were found on the scene. To whom do they belong? Mrs. Daniels and her lunch partner are both possible suspects. Have either of them ever been in trouble before? How do we know?

The homicide detectives had a list of names of clients of the late attorney Daniels, which they ran through the criminal identification section. Soon the fingerprints and criminal records—known as "rap sheets" by criminals and lawmen alike—for each client was in the hands of the detectives. But it wasn't always that easy.

The problems of identification seem straightforward, but they have been a long time in the solving. To better understand the difficulties of criminal identification, and thus better appreciate the solutions that have been found, we will take a short side trip into its history.

IDENTIFICATION BY SCARIFICATION

From medieval Europe to modern times, felons who were not summarily executed—and there were hundreds of crimes for which the penalty was death—were branded. The branding process was insufficiently painful to be considered punishment in an era where the rack, the thumbscrew, and flogging were in common use. It was for identification and was considered merely a method of warning good citizens to beware the offender. In France, beginning in the fourteenth century, the fleur de lis was branded on the shoulder of released convicts. In eighteenth-century Britain, thieves who escaped being hanged were branded on the cheek. In Tsarist Russia, prisoners sent to Siberia were branded on both cheeks and the forehead. The practice did not escape common use until the end of the nineteenth century, and survived in China until 1905.

Another form of identification by disfigurement in use until quite recently in various parts of the world was mutilation, usually involving ear or nose cropping. For many centuries China practiced tattooing, amputation of the nose or feet, and castration. The practice of cutting off a thief's hand, still the law in Iraq, Saudi Arabia, and some other Arab states, serves the triple function of identification, punishment, and crime prevention, but is perhaps a bit arbitrary for less authoritarian regimes.

Branding and mutilation were generic and not very satisfactory solutions. One would know that a person sporting a brand or a V cut into his left earlobe was a felon, but there was still no way to identify which felon he was. A positive means of identifying a specific criminal was needed, though it would be many centuries before that means was found. In the time of the Roman Empire, letters describing missing criminals and runaway slaves were sent out focusing on many of the same details found in the *portrait parlé* developed by Bertillon (see p.117) and used by the police today. But these letters were no more accurate than the powers of observation and description of the writer.

With the growth of cities in the nineteenth century and the establishment of professional police forces in these cities, it became necessary to be able to properly identify the miscreants being sought. An immediate problem was one of a policeman being able to accurately describe a fleeing felon to his mates. But there were longer-range problems as well. Along with the professionalization of the police came the growth in the use of penitentiaries as the preferred method of rehabilitation. But many convicts, after serving their term, would again break the law. The idea grew that these repeat offenders were insufficiently penitent and should receive harsher sentences the second time around. Naturally, professional criminals facing these harsher sentences would refuse to admit their true identity and would go to extreme lengths not to be identified.

Policemen and particularly detectives were encouraged to go to weekly criminal parades, where all the suspects in custody were lined up, and stare at the faces of those passing through the system so that they might recognize them when they ran across them again. Visiting policemen from other jurisdictions were expected to attend the local lineups so they could memorize the features of local criminals and spot any felons wanted on outstanding warrants in their own city. In New York City the detectives attending the lineups wore masks so that the criminals could not return the compliment by recognizing them.

But visual inspection is not a trustworthy method of identification. Many college-level psychology courses demonstrate the dangers of eyewitness testimony with a test like this: someone unexpectedly runs into the class, fires a revolver, and then runs out (or performs some other attention-grabbing stunt). The professor will then ask the students to describe the actions and the actor. Seldom does anyone get all the salient facts right.

It is not just in the classroom that eyewitness testimony is proved problematic. In 1803 a New York City carpenter named Thomas Hoag, happily married and the father of a young daughter, suddenly disappeared. Two years later his sister-in-law heard his distinctive, lisping voice on the street behind her. Turning, she saw that the man behind her was indeed Hoag. She pointed him out to the authorities, and he was arrested for deserting his family. At his trial, eight people—including his landlord, his employer, and a close friend—identified him. He had a scar from when a horse had kicked him in the forehead and a recognizable wen on the back of his neck.

The defendant insisted that it was all a horrible coincidence, that he was one Joseph Parker, even going so far as to bring in eight witnesses of his own, including a wife of eight years to prove it. The judge couldn't decide.

Hoag's friend, with whom he used to exercise daily, remembered that Hoag had a large knife-scar on the bottom of his foot. The defendant was requested to take off his boots, which he gladly did. There was no scar. Parker went home to his wife. Hoag, as far as is known, was never found.

VIDOCQ ON IDENTIFICATION

Eugéne Vidocq, the reformed felon who became head of the Paris police in the 1820s, realized the importance of personal identification. In his memoir he wrote:

I was no sooner the principal agent of the police of safety, than, most jealous of the proper fulfillment of the duty confided to me, I devoted myself seriously to acquire the necessary information. It seemed to me an excellent method to class, as accurately as possible, the descriptions of all the individuals at whom the finger of justice was pointed. I could thereby more readily recognize them if they should escape, and at the expiration of the sentence it became more easy for me to have that surveillance over them that was required of me. I then solicited from M. Henry authority to go to Bicetre with my auxiliaries, that I might examine, during the operation of fettering, both the convicts of Paris and those from the provinces, who generally assemble on the same chain.

Eyewitness identification has not become more reliable with the passage of time. In 1981 John Demjanjuk, a sixty-two-year-old Ukrainian who emigrated to Cleveland, Ohio, in 1952 and worked as a steelworker, lost his United States citizenship for supposedly entering the United States under false pretenses. In 1986 he was extradited to Israel to stand trial for major war crimes. He was accused of being Ivan the Terrible, a guard at the Treblinka death camp who operated the gas chamber and was responsible for the deaths of tens of thousands of Jews during World War II. In 1988, after the highly emotional testimony of Treblinka survivors who identified Demjanjuk as the monstrous guard, and despite his vehement denials of the identification, he was convicted and sentenced to death; a punishment that in Israel is reserved for crimes against humanity.

In 1993 the Israeli Supreme Court reversed the conviction. New evidence from the Soviet archives showed that while Demjanjuk was probably a guard at Sobibor, another death camp in Poland (which the accused denies with equal vehemence), he was never at Treblinka and was not Ivan the Terrible. The survivors' identification of Demjanjuk as the terrible guard they had seen under incredibly stressful conditions forty years before, although made in good faith, was mistaken. He may indeed have been guilty of war crimes, but not of those charged against him.

LORD WILLOUGHBY

A serious case of mistaken identity occurred in Great Britain in 1877. A man calling himself "Lord Willoughby" went to prison for defrauding what the authorities of the time referred to as "women of loose character." Since he was clearly not entitled to the name he claimed, the prison records settled on "John Smith" as a suitable identifier.

In 1894, less than a year after he was released from prison, a cluster of women "mostly of loose character" complained to the police that they had been defrauded by a man calling himself "Lord Wilton," or on occasion, "Lord Winton de Willoughby." The description of the man involved varied, but the bad checks the women had received all seemed to have been written in the same hand. About a year later, on December 16, 1895, one of the ladies, Ottilie Maissonier, passed a Norwegian mining engineer named Adolf Beck on Victoria Street in London. She recognized Beck as Lord Winton de Willoughby, and reported him to a policeman.

Beck protested his innocence, and the bobby took them both back to the police station. Several other similarly defrauded women came to look at Beck and also identified him as the bogus lord. A retired police constable who had dealt with the earlier "John Smith" was called in to look at Beck, and he as well swore that Beck and Smith were one and the same. The constable's opinion was confirmed by a second officer.

Beck was convicted and sentenced to seven years in prison, a harsher sentence than he would otherwise have received for a similar offense, as he was listed in the criminal record books as a repeat offender. In 1896 Beck's lawyer managed to have the case reexamined on the grounds that the prison's own records showed that Smith had been circumcised, whereas Beck had not. Beck was not granted a new trial, even though the evidence of a prior conviction on a like offense must have weighed heavily with the jury, but the court did order his previous conviction expunged from the prison records.

After he had served his term and had been a free man for almost three years, the unfortunate Beck was arrested again on new complaints that read a lot like the old ones. This time he could not protest that he had not previously served time, so he was convicted and sentenced as a repeat offender. But just as Beck was about to be sent away to prison, a man calling himself Thomas was charged with offenses much like those for which Beck had been convicted. When confronted with Thomas, the women who had identified Beck realized that they had made a mistake. The police brought in witnesses to both earlier crimes, and Thomas was identified as the man who had committed the crimes of which Beck had been convicted. Beck was at once granted a "free pardon," and awarded £5,000 in compensation.

PHOTOGRAPHY

The need for an infallible means of identifying those who for whatever reason were in the hands of the police was evident, and the invention of photography brought that goal one step closer. As early as 1854 Daguerreotype photographs of criminals were being taken in Switzerland. A delicate process using wet plates and exposure times of up to several minutes, the procedure must have been trying on both the authorities and the suspects. In the 1860s Paris Commissioner of Police Léon Renault set up the first photographic studio specifically for police use. By the 1880s, with the development of easier-to-use dry-plate photographic processes by R. L. Maddox and Charles Bennett in England and George Eastman in the United States, photography became an essential tool of the police. Pictures of criminals were taken either upon apprehension or conviction, depending on the local laws. Photographs of habitual criminals were gathered together in large books commonly known as the "rogues gallery," which were regularly studied by police. A detective's ability to memorize the faces of habitual criminals in his district was his most useful tool in crime detection and prevention.

Unfortunately, photographs did not prove as reliable as had been initially assumed. First offenders who happened to resemble habitual criminals often were given harsher sentences: In 1888 a convict in Manchester Prison serving a light sentence with lenient treatment as a first offender murdered a warder. In the investigation it was found that he was a known vicious criminal whose appearance had changed sufficiently to fool the camera.

BERTILLON AND THE *PORTRAIT PARLÉ*

The next major step toward a scientifically rigorous means of criminal identification was taken by Alphonse Bertillon, a records clerk in the Paris Prefecture of Police in 1879. His job made him aware of the problem, and his background suggested a possible solution. Bertillon was born in 1853 in Paris. His father, Louis-Adolphe, a medical doctor as well as an anthropologist and statistician, was also a colleague of anthropologist Paul Broca. Broca's research into the human brain first located the speech center and clearly established that many of the mind's functions were at specific locations within the brain.

The young police clerk, aware of the great need for a means of identifying felons and having an intimate knowledge of the human skull from his childhood association with his father and Broca, saw a way to put these together with the theories of Belgian statistician L. A. Quetelet. Quetelet's observation was that there are no two people of exactly the same size. Bertillon realized that if the statistician's theory was indeed so, then it was only necessary to measure two people in order to tell them apart. And if a record of such measurements was kept, a person could be identified with certainty if there ever were the occasion to measure him again.

The three basic tenets of the system Bertillon worked out—a system he called anthropometrics, but which his French compatriots called *Bertillonage*—were:

1. That after about age twenty, the underlying bone structure of the human body is fixed.

2. That if one picked the right measurements, one could differentiate the entire human race.

3. That these measurements can be taken with sufficient precision and without great difficulty.

On December 13, 1882, Prefect of Police Jean Camescasse gave Bertillon authority to conduct a three-month trial of his system. Two months and one week later, on February 20, 1883, Bertillon identified his first recidivist; the trial was promptly extended. During 1883 Bertillon's anthropometric system identified forty-three recidivists, and in 1884 the number rose to 241. These successes were so impressive that a new service of judicial identity was formed, and Bertillon was placed at its head.

The system that Bertillon developed had three components:

1. Measurements of the body: height of subject standing, reach (fingertip to fingertip with the arms outstretched), height of subject sitting (trunk).

2. Measurements of the head: maximum length front-to-rear ("antero-posterior"), breadth ("transverse maximum cranial diameter"), length and bizygomatical diameter of the right ear.

3. Measurement of the limbs: length of the left foot; length of the left middle and little fingers; length of the left forearm from the elbow to the tip of the middle finger.

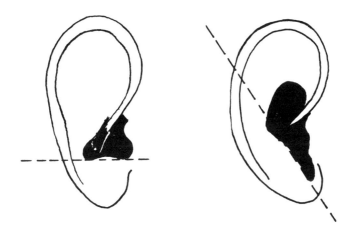

BERTILLON MEASURED THE LENGTH AND BIZYGO-
MATICAL DIAMETER OF THE RIGHT EAR.

The left side was picked for limb measurements because it was felt that it was less subject to change due to the stress of physical work, as most people were right-handed.

Bertillon had special chairs constructed to standardize the measuring process, along with special calipers for measuring the skull and the ear. Nonetheless the personnel taking the measurements had to be trained to do it right or the results would be anything but uniform. Even in the best of situations the measurements would vary from one taker to another and from one time to another. Bertillon was forced to publish a table of tolerances to allow for such errors. Another constant problem was the number of criminals under twenty years old, whose anthropometric measurements were still subject to the changes of maturity.

These records would be useless without a means of locating a specific record for comparison. French criminalist Edmond Locard described the system that was devised thus:

> The mass of a service's files is divided into three groups, according to whether the length of the head is large, medium, or small. Each of the groups is divided into three subgroups according to the breadth of the head. Then each subgroup in its turn is subdivided into three classes by the length of the middle finger. And each class of middle fingers into three categories by the length of the ring finger.

After a short while Bertillon found it expedient to add a fourth element: a pair of photographs, full and profile, taken with a special camera, attached to a verbal description, called a *portrait parlé,* which included such items as birthmarks, scars, tattoos, and noticeable deformities. The *portrait parlé* was also meant to stand alone, to be used as a verbal identification system—a policeman trained in the procedure could theoretically recognize one person in a crowd from the written description. But with hundreds of possible subdivisions and fine details, it took time and intelligence to master. As originally devised by Bertillon there were four major sections to the portrait:

1. Determination of color of left eye, hair, beard, and skin.

2. Morphological description of the various parts of the head, with emphasis on the right ear.

3. General considerations—body shape, carriage, voice and language or accent, clothing, apparent social standing, etc.
4. Indelible markings; scars, tattoos, birthmarks, and the like.

WANTED

Before the advent of the photograph and the *portrait parlé,* which could narrow down the possibilities to about ten people in a thousand, the descriptions the police used left most of the thousand at risk.

Toward the end of June 1897 the body of William Guldensuppe, a rubber in the Murray Hill Turkish Baths on 42nd Street, was found in various places around Greater New York, the bulk of it in three different packages floating in the Hudson and East Rivers. The police soon had a suspect and sent out a general alarm for his apprehension with the following bulletin:

Wanted—For the murder of William Guldensuppe. Martin Thorn, whose right name is Martin Torczewski, born in Posen, Germany; 33 to 34 years old; about 5 feet 8 inches in height, weighs about 155 pounds, has blue-gray eyes, very dark hair, red cheeks, and light brown mustache, thick and curled at the ends. Has a small scar on the forehead. Speaks with a slight German accent. Is an expert pinochle player and a first-class barber.

Although the crime created much excitement, and several men throughout the United States and Canada were arrested on suspicion of being Thorn, the real suspect eluded detection for more than a week, spending his time playing pinochle in a saloon frequented by policemen fewer than fifty yards from the 34th Street Ferry entrance. He avoided recognition by the simple expedient of shaving off his "light brown mustache," and was only caught when a friend, who feared for his own life, turned Thorn in.

The *portrait parlé* has been modified over the years into the simpler and more-or-less uniform identification form used today by most police forces. One version of this form, used by police departments to this day (as given in Söderman and O'Connell's book *Modern Criminal Investigation*), looks like this:

```
NAME . . .

SEX . . .

COLOR . . .

NATIONALITY . . .

OCCUPATION . . .

AGE . . .

HEIGHT . . .

WEIGHT . . .

BUILD—Large; stout or very stout; medium; slim; stooped
or square-shouldered; stocky.

COMPLEXION—Florid; sallow; pale; fair; dark.

HAIR—Color; thick or thin; bald or partly bald; curly;
kinky; wavy; how cut or parted; style of hair dress.

EYES—Color of the iris; eyes bulgy or small; any pecu-
liarities.

EYEBROWS—Slanting, up or down; bushy or meeting; arched,
wavy, horizontal; as to texture: strong; thin; short- or
long-haired; penciled.

NOSE—Small or large; pug, hooked, straight, flat.

WHISKERS—Color; Vandyke; straight; rounded; chin whis-
kers; goatee; side whiskers.

MUSTACHE—Color; short; stubby; long; pointed ends;
turned-up ends; Kaiser style.

CHIN—Small, large; square; dimpled; double; flat;
arched.

FACE—Long; round; square; peg-top; fat; thin.

NECK—Long; short; thick; thin; folds in back of neck;
puffed neck; prominent Adam's apple.

LIPS—Thick; thin; puffy; drooping lower; upturned upper.
```

MOUTH—Large; small; drooping or upturned at corners; open; crooked; distorted during speech or laughter; contorted.

HEAD—Posture of: bent forward; turned sideways; to left or right; inclined backward or to left or right.

EARS—Small; large; close to or projecting out from head; pierced.

FOREHEAD—High; low; sloping; bulging; straight; receding.

DISTINCTIVE MARKS—Scars; moles; missing fingers or teeth; gold teeth; tattoo marks; lameness; bow legs; pigeon toes; knock-knees; cauliflower ears; pockmarked; flat feet; nicotine fingers; freckles; birthmarks.

PECULIARITIES—Twitching of features; rapid or slow gait; long or short steps; wearing of eyeglasses; carrying a cane; stuttering; gruff or effeminate voice.

CLOTHES—Hat and shoes: color and style; suit: color; cut; maker's name; shirt and collar: style and color; tie: style and color; dressed neatly or carelessly.

JEWELRY—Kind of; where worn.

WHERE LIKELY TO BE FOUND—Residence; former residences; places frequented or hangouts; where employed; residences of relatives, etc.

PERSONAL ASSOCIATES—Friends who would be most likely to know of the movements or whereabouts of the person wanted, or with whom he would be most likely to communicate.

HABITS—Heavy drinker or smoker; drug addiction; gambler; frequenter of pool parlors; dance halls; cabarets; baseball games; resorts, etc.

HOW HE LEFT THE SCENE OF THE CRIME—Running; walking; by vehicle; direction taken.

In complexion, the recorder is to note peculiarities such as freckles, pockmarks, and the like. The hair could be light blond, blond, dark blond, brown, black, red, white, mixed gray, or gray. Baldness is also to be noted, and described as either frontal, occipital, top of head, or full. Eyes are either blue, gray, maroon, yellow, light brown, brown, or dark brown. There are also various notable peculiarities such as extreme bloodshotness, eyes of two different colors, and *arcus senilis* (a white ring around the edge of the cornea).

FRONTAL, OCCIPITAL, AND TOP OF HEAD BALDNESS

The shape of the nose was of prime importance until recently, but now that rhinoplasty has become as common as tonsillectomy, it can no longer be trusted. It is by the ear that one may know the man. Its shape is changeless—barring accident—from birth to death and is the surest means of confirming identification by photograph.

The ear varies from person to person in its position and angle on the head and in the angle it sticks out from the head. It may take one of four different general shapes: round, oval, rectangular, or triangular. It is divided into six parts, the helix, the antihelix, the tragus, the antitragus, the lobule and the concha. The helix is further subdivided, may be either folded or flat, and can form a variety of angles. The other parts also have their distinctive peculiarities, which when combined make tens of thousands of possible different ears. A large enough number for preliminary elimination, but not large enough for positive identification.

The United States Immigration and Naturalization Service still has a lot of faith in the ear. The photograph used by the INS on the Resident Alien ID card is taken with the subject's head turned a quarter toward the left, so that the right ear is showing. Any hair or jewelry in the way is moved aside for the photograph.

Bertillon advanced the science of identification photography with a system called metric photography, involving standardization of the camera, the lens, the distance from the camera to the subject, and the chair the subject is seated in. He suggested a standardized reduction of 1:7 for all photographs, so the relative sizes of the heads would be immediately apparent. Bertillon also pointed out something that should not have needed mentioning—that the photographic negative should not be retouched to remove scars or blemishes from the subject's face.

Bertillon also devised a method of improving the use of the camera to photograph crime scenes which involved the use of standardized lenses, the taking of pictures from standardized heights above the floor, and the process of printing the images on special paper with either an indoor or outdoor grid already printed on it.

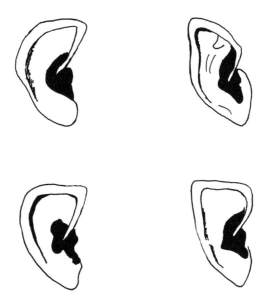

THE HUMAN EAR IN SOME OF ITS INFINITE VARIETIES.

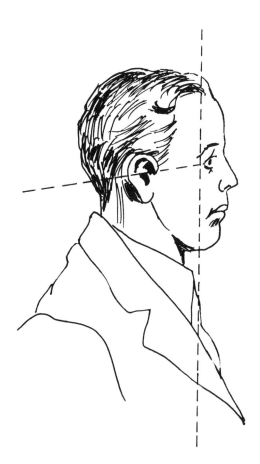

THE RIGHT SIDE OF THE FACE, INCLUDING THE EAR, AS
IT SHOULD BE VIEWED FOR A BERTILLON PHOTOGRAPH.

The anthropometric system, the *portrait parlé,* and metric photography were great steps forward in the history of criminalistics. Bertillon also made lesser but still important advances, such as the "galvanoplastic" method of preserving footprints found at the scene of the crime.

While Bertillon was identifying criminals by the measurements of their heads, Italian criminologist Cesare Lombroso, director of an insane asylum in Pesaro, Italy, took this one step further—though in which direction it's hard to say. Misunderstanding the theory of evolution, Lombroso decided that criminals were different from their more law-abiding brethren because they had either atavistic or degenerative traits. Those who were atavistic were throwbacks to an earlier step of evolution, while those who were degenerative were progressing in the wrong direction along the evolutionary line.

Both types would show physical anomalies which would make it possible to recognize them even if the subjects had not yet committed the criminal acts that their nature had doomed them to. The atavists could be recognized by their subhuman characteristics, "reminiscent of apes and lower primates, which occur in the more simian fossil men, and are to some extent retained in modern savages." The degenerates, in turn, could be identified by their congenital weaknesses and their general slackjawed, unintelligent look. Lombroso also felt that tattooing, unless extremely minor, was a symptom of degeneracy. The criminologist used Bertillon's anthropometric techniques to collect measurements of his "criminal types," and found what he deemed a meaningful correlation. Bertillon returned Lombroso's compliment, firmly embracing the theories of Lombroso. Bartillion's student, H. Ashton-Wolfe, explained that:

> Criminal faces, as the police and the laboratory experts understand them, are divided into three sections: those of degenerates or throw-backs, which vary little during their lifetime; those stamped with the evil characteristics which a career of crime inevitably evolves through constant association with others of the species and a frequent sojourn in penal establishments; and, finally, the faces which reveal Darwinian deformation and asymmetry of the features which,

in many instances, may be merely some single strikingly abnormal development due to hereditary criminal tendencies.

Bertillon, who seems to have had an ear fixation, decided that an infallible sign of atavism or degeneration was a "striking asymmetry and malformation of the ears." Lombroso's later contention that genius was another form of degeneracy eventually brought him into disrepute.

NOTHING BUT THE TEETH

Forensic odontology or forensic dentistry is an important tool for identifying the remains of the long dead or corpses that have been mutilated or burned beyond recognition. It is especially useful in cases where the fingerprints are missing or unrecognizable. Every catastrophe involving loss of life will see a forensic odontologist as a member of the investigation team, for teeth are—as some creative murderers have found to their dismay—extremely resistant to destruction by fire or the action of chemical corrosives.

The normal practice of dentistry demands the keeping of accurate records of any additions to or subtractions from the normal complement and construction of the teeth. And as most people in this country will have gone to a dentist at some time, their dental records will be somewhere to be found. In cases where no dental records can be located, DNA fingerprinting can now be used on the interior pulp of the teeth for confirming identity (see chapter seven).

If a body must be examined for identification and a forensic odontologist is not available or will be delayed in arriving, the technician on the scene should describe the jaw and teeth in her notes. If extensive wounding has occurred in the vicinity of the face, the dental examination should probably wait until after the pathologist has examined the body, so as not to inadvertently cause post-mortem injuries.

A sketch should be made of the upper and lower jaw, noting first of all which teeth are present; dentists have well-designed forms often used for this. The condition of each tooth present should then be noted, including describing any cracks, chips, holes, caries (cavities), missing or damaged fillings, or crowns. The color of the teeth—from sparkling white to dark brown—should be noted, as should the amount of wear, and the dental work present should be described as best as possible. Dentures should be described and carefully examined for inscriptions; many have engraved somewhere on them the name of the maker, the doctor, the group or service, or even a prison inmate number. A forensic odontologist will be able to add to this information with x-rays of the jaw, enabling him to describe dental work such as root canals or deep fillings that may not be evident on the surface. It is also possible to make a good estimate of the age of the deceased by observing the state of certain characteristic time-related changes in the dentation, such as the eruption of wisdom teeth.

THE EYEWITNESS

Despite the unreliability of eyewitness testimony, the descriptions of perpetrators given by victims or witnesses can be very helpful to a pending investigation. The fact that such testimony is not always reliable does not mean that it is always wrong. The criminalist must be aware, however, that an honest identification given by an intelligent, perceptive, and upright citizen might be entirely mistaken. If there is more than one witness, the examiner should be careful to question each witness separately. Many psychological experiments have verified that people are very suggestible, and that their memory of an event can actually be subtly altered so that it agrees with someone else's verbal description without their being aware of the process.

For this reason it is also very important to ask the questions in as neutral a manner as possible. If the investigator asks, "Was the man in the brown car tall or short?" that might be enough to fix in the witness's mind that the car was brown, even if it was blue. The next person who asks the witness about the color of the car will be told that it was brown, and the witness will not realize that the answer came from a previous questioner instead of from his own experience.

This phenomenon is especially true with small children, so their testimony concerning a series of events must always be carefully evaluated, especially if some adult has, perhaps with the best of intentions, discussed their memory of the events with them before the investigator has had a chance to question them.

A physical description of the criminal can help tremendously, if only to eliminate suspects, but the investigator must be cautious in the elimination. Many times a perpetrator who was described in all good faith by a witness as being a short man in a dark suit has turned out to be a tall woman in a light dress. The most positive identification is when the victim or witness actually knows the offender. "It was my husband," or "It was Uncle Charles," or even, "It was the lady who runs the cat-clipping store on Third Street" is a good, positive identification, much better than having to pick someone out of a book of photographs whom the witness has seen only briefly.

Cross-cultural identifications are especially difficult. This has nothing to do with whether the witness has a prejudice against the race or culture in question, but is an artifact of the way our memory works. We subconsciously look for visual cues to peg the identity. So although everyone in Sweden can tell each other apart, to a person raised among short, dark-haired Corsicans, all tall blond Swedes look alike. If you have ever approached a total stranger, convinced that it was a good friend until you got close enough to make out the fine details of the person's features, then you may understand. It may have been a manner of walking, or a trick of holding the head, that you had never consciously realized you identified with your friend.

Many police departments utilize sketch artists, technicians who have been trained in gathering the descriptive information and putting it on paper while influencing the witness's description as little as possible. Faces can now also be re-created using specially designed computer programs as well as identification kits utilizing overlays of eyes, ears, noses, and hairstyles on a variety of different head shapes. Sometimes these technologies have done an amazing job of reproducing the face in question, but identification kit simulations have a lifeless quality that makes it difficult to "see" the subject, even when the likeness is fairly close.

Armed with the information from the records section, the Gotham City homicide detectives go forth to investigate all those who as clients of a criminal lawyer might have had reason to wish him harm. The investigation quickly turns up an unknown aspect of Daniels's business dealings: Several of his clients have made it clear that the attorney did a little fencing on the side and was known for sharp dealing with his customers.

One of these ex-clients, a gentleman burglar known as Philomar "The Yegg" Yancy, has drawn the attention of the detectives to himself by being lately absent from his usual haunts. It is a well-known maxim of the police that a felon in hiding is one who has something to hide.

SEVEN

IT'S IN THE BLOOD

> *He stood there above the body,*
> *He stood there holding the knife;*
> *And the blood ran down the stairs and sang:*
> *'I'm the Resurrection and the Life'.*

W. H. AUDEN,
VICTOR

> *Examine well your blood . . .*

WILLIAM SHAKESPEARE,
A MIDSUMMER NIGHT'S DREAM

The Gotham City forensic team went to work on the possible bloodstains in Godfrey Daniels's study after his body was removed. Portions of the suspected stains were sprayed with a blood-revealing chemical, which showed a positive result. Unfortunately various substances other than blood also cause a positive reaction, so the exemplars were removed and carefully packaged for transmittal to the crime laboratory for further analysis. The water in the trap in the bathroom sink drain had also tested positive for the presence of blood, but there was probably too little to gather any positive information.

The criminalists went over the study carefully and were especially careful to get samples of any stain that looked as if it might not have originated with Mr. Daniels. An expert on blood-splatter interpretation looked over the room; he said that Daniels had been sitting behind his desk when he was shot, and then had probably gone around the desk himself, possibly in an attempt to grapple with his assailant. The blood-splatter pattern indicated that the killer had himself been wounded, though probably superficially. The splatter expert indicated to the technicians which of the stains had probably come from the killer's wound. If there was enough blood to type in these exemplars, it might go a long way toward identifying the killer.

Blood has always been an object of awe. Though its function was poorly understood until this century, its evident importance in maintaining life has always given it a mystical quality: If your "life's blood" ebbs out, you will die; patriots are "red-blooded Americans"; the nobility are "blue bloods." The "bloodlines" of an animal—or a person—denote breeding, and thus quality. An evil person has "bad blood"; an insane person has "tainted blood"; and a person of a race other than your own has "inferior blood." Blood, after all, is thicker than water.

Blood is quite often found at the site of a murder and, although "blood will tell," for centuries such splashes and clots at a crime scene stayed mute. Then, about the middle of the last century, blood began giving up its forensic secrets.

Nineteenth-century improvements to the microscope brought the discovery that blood consists of a thin fluid, called blood serum, in which travel red and white blood cells by the millions. These cells, if identified microscopically, would be an infallible test for blood. But if the stains were too small or too old, they were difficult to identify. Then in 1863, Christian Schönbein, a German scientist, discovered that blood causes a strong reaction when introduced to hydrogen peroxide. Over the next half-century other reagents were discovered that were even more sensitive, most reacting to hemoglobin, the oxygen-carrying compound in blood. With extensive improvements in technology, even the smallest trace of blood can now be identified, and it takes only slightly more to be able to identify the blood as human and to type it—the process of discovering its specific factors that limit the number of people it could have come from. Moreover, with DNA analysis, a blood sample now is as distinctive as a fingerprint, as we will see in the next chapter.

There are three questions that the crime scene investigator needs to have answered about suspicious stains: Are they blood? Are they human blood? And does the blood from each stain come from the victim or the murderer? These questions have a particular urgency when the stains in question are on a suspect's clothing. If a stain proves to be some substance other than blood, then a whole other set of questions will come into play.

Liquid blood dries fairly quickly, clotting first on the surface exposed to air and then continuing to dry from the outside in. It is this propensity of blood to clot, a fairly complex chemical and biological process, that prevents us from bleeding to death following minor cuts or bruises. Liquid blood is thin and light red in color. Newly clotted blood turns a darker red, shading to red-brown. A dried bloodstain can be any number of colors, from black to transparent, including brown, blue, green, grey, and white. The color is determined by the physical and chemical composition of the surface upon which the blood falls, the thickness of the stain itself, and outside factors such as temperature, humidity, and sunlight. Attempts to remove bloodstains are quite often less than completely successful, and the presence of blood can often be detected even after the criminal has scrubbed, washed, bleached, and scraped in an attempt to conceal or remove it.

In examining for bloodstains, especially when it is suspected that the criminal may have cleaned up after the crime, the forensic technician must be diligent, thorough, and imaginative. The miscreant may have scrubbed all the obvious places, but forgotten that he touched the underside of the washbasin or the inside of a bureau drawer with a hand still sticky with his victim's blood. With luck the investigator can get both a bloodstain and a fingerprint in one incriminating mark.

If the criminal washed his hands, there may be blood caught in the trap in the sink drain. The criminalist will unscrew the drain plug and save the water for testing. If a wooden floor has been well-scrubbed recently—in itself a suspicious circumstance unless the premises are occupied by a fanatical house-cleaner—the cracks between the floorboards may still harbor traces of blood.

When checking for bloodstains in the field, the forensic investigator has a variety of tests at her disposal. The beam of light from a strong flashlight held at an acute angle to the floor or wall may illuminate stains that would otherwise pass notice. The benzidine test, a highly sensitive test for the presence of blood (which unfortunately also tests positive for fresh fruit and milk), has fallen out of favor as benzidine has been shown to be a powerful carcinogen. It has been replaced by orthotolidine, a chemical relative which is just as sensitive but safer to use.

The reduced phenolphthalein test is used as an alternate to benzidine or orthotolidine. Like them, it suffers from the problem of false positive: If the liquid in which the sample is dropped does not turn rose colored (the phenolphthalein reaction), it definitely is not blood. If it does turn rose colored, then the substance may be blood, or it may be one of a number of other things.

One of the oldest and most sensitive tests is the leuco malachite test, in which a reagent is made up of a chemical called leuco malachite green mixed with acetic acid and distilled water. Shortly before it is to be used, a solution of hydrogen peroxide is added to the reagent. A sample of the suspect stain is then scraped (where possible) onto a piece of filter paper, and a drop of the mixture is added. If the suspect stain is indeed blood, the mixture will turn green (the leuco malachite solution is already slightly green), and the color will darken over the first minute or so. The test is so sensitive that great care must be taken that the instruments used—the blade used to scrape the stain, the filter paper, and the glass rod used to move a drop of the solution to the test area—are free of any trace of blood from a previous test. A careful technician will test the mixture first, both alone and on a known drop of old blood, to make sure it reacts when, and only when, it is supposed to.

The luminol test can detect traces of blood overlooked by other tests or in places where efforts have been made to clean up. This test is successful because blood reacts with luminol (a mixture of sodium carbonate, sodium perborate, and 3-aminophthalhydrazide) by luminescing: The room to be tested is darkened, the technician waits for her eyes to adjust to the dim light, and then luminol is sprayed on the locations to be examined. If traces of blood are present, a faint blue glow will be detected where the blood has reacted with the reagent. The more blood present, the stronger and brighter the glow. Oddly, old blood reacts more strongly than fresh blood to this test.

If a stain tests positive for blood in the field, it will, where possible, be taken to the crime laboratory for further testing, since all such field tests may react to a substance other than blood. If the blood sample is still liquid, it can be preserved by transferring it to a test tube containing a saline solution of distilled water plus slightly less than 1 percent sodium chloride (table salt). This best preserves the red blood cells in something approaching a natural state. If a suitably prepared test tube is not available, then the blood sample can be soaked up onto a sterile piece of filter paper, a cotton swab, or a piece of cotton fabric. All of these must be known to be scrupulously clean beforehand or the test results will be meaningless.

In the case of small stains on clothing, furniture, or objects in the room, the entire object can be removed from the crime scene (when the other investigators and the photographer have finished) and brought to the lab. In the cases of blood on the floor or wall, whole sections of the structure can be, and have been, sawed out and brought into the laboratory for examination. They are also often saved and mounted for use as exhibits at the trial. If a sample believed to contain blood is cut from a large object like a carpet, from the upholstery of a couch, or from a mattress, a sample should also be taken from an area that is not blood-stained as a control, to ensure that there is nothing in the makeup of the material that would cause a false positive reading.

The clothing of the victim may be removed at the crime scene if necessary to preserve bloodstain evidence. If the clothing must be cut from the victim, the technician must be careful not to further damage any existing cuts, rips, tears, bullet or knife holes, or any of the bloody areas. If the clothing is still wet or damp, it should be spread out to dry and not folded or rolled up, as this might transfer an existing stain to another location. All urges to clean the clothing, or even brush it off, must be rejected, and the clothing should be delivered to the crime laboratory in as close to the condition it was found as possible. Each piece of clothing should be wrapped separately, possibly in wrapping paper with no printing on it.

In a crime scene containing a battered and bloody victim, the inclination is to assume that all the blood present came from the victim, but this may not be so. If the victim fought back, or if the perpetrator scratched his hand or had a nosebleed, there may be samples of the perpetrator's blood in among the sanguinary exemplars from the victim. Finding and identifying these might go a long way toward discovering the identity of the criminal and successfully prosecuting him, so the crime scene should be carefully examined with this in mind. Several, or if necessary many, samples of blood should be taken for identification.

The natural impulse in removing a sample from a bloodstain would be to encapsulate it in some way: to bottle it, wrap it in plastic, or seal it in a plastic bag. Unfortunately this would cause a blood sample (or one of semen, saliva, or other biological fluid) to deteriorate rapidly. Many a well-meaning but untrained police officer has inadvertently rendered evidence useless in an attempt to preserve it. Many jurisdictions have specific regulations regarding how biological evidence is to be handled. The basic rule is to refrigerate or freeze it as quickly as possible. The specimen still won't last forever, but it will last considerably longer this way.

When a sample is brought into the crime laboratory, the only thing that has been established is that it is probably blood—or that it isn't. For the samples that are thought to be blood, a series of tests are performed; first to establish that it is indeed blood, and then to discover just what sort of blood it is.

If the stain is recent it can be examined under a microscope, and the presence of red blood cells will confirm that it is blood. If the stain is a bit older, a wide variety of tests may be used, according to the practice of the individual laboratory. Each has its advantages and disadvantages, but all are capable of establishing beyond doubt that the sample being tested is blood. A spectrographic analysis of a small sample will show the characteristic spectrum of hemoglobin or one of its breakdown products. Unfortunately the spectrum for each of the breakdown products is different, and sometimes the complexity of the resulting spectrogram makes a proper reading of the results difficult or impossible.

The precipitin reaction test will not only verify that the substance is blood but will tell what sort of animal the blood came from.

BUT IS HE YOUR SPECIES?

There is a visible difference under the microscope between the blood of mammals (which includes us) and the blood of other vertebrates (just about all other animals). The two major components of blood, besides the serum, which is an analog of the seawater that our ancestors crawled out of a few millennia ago, are red and white blood cells. The white cells are scavengers, destroying and removing bacteria and other foreign agents that invade our bloodstreams. The red blood cells pick up oxygen from the lungs (or gills if you're a fish) and transport it to the body's cells, which use it to produce energy. It is these red blood cells that differs visibly under the microscope. Non-mammals have oval red blood cells with a visible nucleus, while mammalian red blood cells have no nucleus and are circular (except, for some reason, those of camels and llamas, which are elliptical). Unfortunately for forensic science, this difference can only be detected when the blood is fresh; as blood dries its cells clump and lose their shape.

Even if the blood is fresh enough to be shown to be mammalian blood, there is the question of what sort of mammal contributed the bloodstain to the crime scene.

In the mid-nineteenth century a French scientist named Barreul became convinced that he could identify the source animal of a bloodstain from the blood's odor. Cow's blood, he maintained, when boiled in sulfuric acid, smelled like the inside of a barn. Human blood similarly treated smelled like human sweat. When other people couldn't detect the odors, however, this promising development was abandoned.

A reliable means of differentiating the species of a blood sample was discovered in 1900 by a German serologist named Paul Uhlenhuth. He was following up on the discovery made a decade before by Emil von Behring that if a small quantity of diphtheria toxin was injected into a rabbit, the rabbit would develop antibodies against diphtheria, and these antibodies helped diphtheria patients recover. What Uhlenhuth discovered was that if he injected chicken egg protein into rabbits, the rabbits' blood sera would develop a sort of antibody against the foreign protein that was highly specific. If the white of an egg was mixed with the treated rabbit serum, a cloudy precipitate would form and drop to the bottom of the test tube—*if it was a chicken egg*. The rabbits' blood sera was very definite. The little white cloud would not form for duck egg protein, or pigeon egg protein, or turkey, or any other.

Uhlenhuth tried the experiment with a variety of other animal proteins and found that the test remained very precise and very specific. Only closely related species could fool the rabbit serum antibodies: Horses and donkeys could not be told apart, and, unfortunately for the anti-evolutionists, neither could humans and chimpanzees or gorillas. Now, if a man claimed that the blood on his pants cuff was from an elk and not from his Great Aunt Matilda who had been found bludgeoned to death, forensic science could test his story. Although if he claimed that his pet chimp had a nosebleed, there would be none who could gainsay him, provided that he could produce the chimp.

We've now established that the stain is blood, and that it is human blood. Can we go further?

In 1900 Viennese doctor Karl Landsteiner discovered that human blood could be divided into four types. These four differed in that the red blood cells of some of the types clumped together when introduced into the serum of another type. This discovery made possible the safe transfusion of blood from one person to another for the first time. The common grouping, which determines whose blood your body will accept in a transfusion, are named types A, B, AB, and O. The differences are in a substance called an agglutinogen contained in the red corpuscles, and a corresponding substance called an agglutinin in the blood serum. The agglutinin in the serum exists to cause red blood cells with the wrong agglutinogen to clump if they somehow enter the body. What the function of this antagonism of one type of blood to another is we do not know, and until it was understood transfusions were a horribly risky business.

The way it works is this: Group A serum will clump group B blood cells; group B serum will clump group A blood cells; neither will clump group O blood cells; and either will clump AB. But group O serum will clump either A or B cells; while AB serum will not clump any cells. What this means to doctors is that people with group O blood are universal donors, but can receive blood only from another group O. Group A people can receive either A or O, group B people can receive either B or O, and group AB can receive from anyone, but can only be donors for other group AB. Because some people have adverse reactions to blood types that the general rules say they should be able to tolerate, it is still better, particularly when the patient must receive large amounts of transfused blood, to match the types as closely as possible. A rough breakdown of the percentages of the blood groups in the general population is

O: 44%
A: 40%
B: 12%
AB: 4%

There are some rare cases of non-identical twins who have combined blood types, presumably because of mixing of placental blood vessels in the womb. One twin in Britain in the 1950s was found to have blood that was 60 percent type O and 40 percent type A. In another case one twin was found to have 86 percent A and 14 percent O, while the other sibling had 99 percent O and 1 percent A. (If any twin so endowed was to commit a crime and leave a bloodstain behind, a forensic serologist who has not heard of this phenomenon would be sorely puzzled.)

Although there are areas of the world where, due to isolation and local inbreeding, the percentage of one blood group may be higher than elsewhere, there is no correspondence between blood groups and the various "races" of mankind.

The value of blood groups to the forensic serologist is in their power to eliminate. No one can be found guilty because his blood group matches that found at the scene of the crime, but suspects can be eliminated because their blood group does not match. Classification, in many cases, can be made even more specific. There are subdivisions of the ABO typing, based on the strength of the agglutinin in the serum of A-type blood, dividing it into A_1 and A_2, and thus A_1B and A_2B. The Rh factor (so called because it is also found in rhesus monkeys), is present in about 85 percent of the population. An important compatibility consideration in pregnancy (an Rh negative woman can develop antibodies against her Rh positive fetus, which could prove fatal to the fetus in a subsequent pregnancy), Rh is also a useful determinant in further subdividing blood types.

Other divisions of blood groups have since been found, such as the M, N, and MN classifications, and there is also a P factor, which may or may not be present. While these are of no practical importance to the doctor or patient, since mixing them does not cause blood to clot, they can be used forensically to further eliminate suspects. And because these various groups are inherited, the laws of genetics have made blood groupings a valuable tool toward establishing doubtful paternity in cases where that fact is disputed or unknown.

THE DELICATE TYPE

As analytical methods have improved, a variety of other blood differences have been noted in the recent past, in addition to the ABO blood groupings, the MN and P classifications, and the Rh factor. Consisting of slight biological changes in the structure of particular proteins or enzymes in the blood, these additional blood types are meaningless for anyone except genetic statisticians and forensic serologists. These new types are differentiated by a technique called electrophoresis: A cotton thread is saturated with the blood sample and embedded in a thin gel which has been spread across a glass plate. A direct current is passed through the gel, which causes the various molecules in the blood to travel down the glass plate at speeds which are slightly different for each protein or enzyme. After a specified length of time, the current is turned off and the glass plate is stained with a substance that will reveal the traveling enzymes, which show up as dark bands at different distances down the plate.

The correct reading of these bands takes skill and training. As the blood gets older, some of these differences fade away and some totally disappear. This is less true of ABO typing, which has been successful in testing the dried blood of mummies several thousand years old; nor is it always true of the

DNA (see chapter eight), which can persist for ages. Direct sunlight, excess heat or moisture, or bloodstains kept moist when saved as evidence can all contribute to the more rapid deterioration of the blood samples, making these delicate differences impossible to discern. DNA testing, which uses an analogous process for the final determination, is much more complex, much more precise, and can take up to two months to finalize the results.

Among the blood grouping systems that are now identifiable are:

Adenosine Deaminase	(ADA)
Adenylate Dinase	(AK)
Erthrocyte Acid Phosphatase	(EAP)
Esterase D	(EsD)
Glyoxalase I	(GLOI)
Group-Specific Component	(Gc)
Haptoglobin	(Hp)
Hemoglobin	(Hb)
Phosphoglucomutase	(PGM)
Transferrin	(Tf)

If these groupings can be determined, the percentage of the population that could be the source of the blood sample can be narrowed to well under 1 percent. This is still not good enough for positive identification, but it is a wonderful tool for elimination of suspects.

In about 60 percent of the population blood typing can also be obtained from a variety of other body fluids, such as saliva, semen, tears, perspiration, or urine. It has been established that once a secretor (as this percentage of people is known), always a secretor, although no one knows why, and that the typing of the secretions will always match the blood type of the individual.

The use of blood grouping, while still a valuable tool for the forensic technician, is being complemented by the newer field of DNA fingerprinting, which can offer near-positive identification instead of merely elimination (*see chapter eight*). However, a DNA test can take from four to six weeks to produce results, and those may still be inconclusive; as a blood-group test can be done in a matter of hours, the technology of blood typing is still useful.

BLOODSTAINS, SPLATTER, AND SPLASH

In addition to blood type, the size, shape, and distribution of bloodstains at a crime scene can be a great aid to the investigator in reconstructing the events of the crime. Blood splatters on the walls and floor can show where the assault happened, the direction of the blows, and the force of the blows. From these, an investigator can be interpolate where the killer and victim were standing, which hand the killer used to strike the victim, whether the victim fought back, and other details that may prove relevant.

THE SAM SHEPPARD CASE

In the early morning hours of July 4, 1954, Bay Village police were called to the home of Dr. Samuel Sheppard, a wealthy and popular osteopathic surgeon. They found an apparently battered and barely coherent Dr. Sam downstairs being tended by the mayor of Bay Village, Sheppard's next-door neighbor, and upstairs in the bedroom the body of Marilyn Sheppard, Dr. Sam's wife, who had been savagely beaten to death.

Bay Village, an exclusive suburb of Cleveland, Ohio, had never experienced a crime remotely like this before. The murder quickly became the subject of intense interest, rapidly heightening to passion. Dr. Sam's story was that he had been sleeping on the living-room couch when he was awakened by the sound of Marilyn screaming upstairs. He rushed upstairs but was knocked down—and out—by a "white figure" on the staircase. The next thing he remembered was waking up on the beach (his house bordered Lake Erie) sometime later. He rushed home and ran upstairs to find Marilyn dead in the bedroom. He came back downstairs and called his next-door neighbor, Mayor John Spencer Houk, and then collapsed on the living-room couch.

Houk and his wife hurriedly dressed—it was around five A.M.—
and rushed over. Houk tried to rouse a confused Sheppard while
Houk's wife went upstairs and found Marilyn Sheppard's mutilated body.

Dr. Sam, whose spine was feared to have been injured, was
taken to the hospital by his brother, a doctor. The investigating
officers found that suspicious, as they did the fact that his story
continued to remain vague—Sheppard couldn't improve on his
description of the "white figure." Why they found his trip to
the hospital (where he was immediately accessible as soon as
authorities wanted him) or his inability to describe an assailant
he saw only in the dark to be suspicious is not known.

The coroner found a bloodstain on the pillowcase under
Marilyn's body that seemed to him to have the shape of a "surgical instrument." The specific instrument could not be
identified, but the term "surgical instrument" seems to have
hypnotized the police. They settled on Sheppard—a surgeon—
as the murderer of his wife, Marilyn. The people of Bay Village
turned against Dr. Sam when they learned that he had a mis-
tress. Although Sam and Marilyn were known to have a happy
marriage, despite possible infidelities on both of their parts,
and no other reason was ever alleged as to why he would want
to beat his wife to death, Dr. Samuel Sheppard was tried and
convicted for the murder of Marilyn Sheppard.

It was not until after Sheppard's conviction that people from
his defense team were allowed to enter the house where the
murder had been committed, which had been under police seal
by order of the coroner. Sheppard's lawyer, William J. Corrigan,
asked Dr. Paul Leland Kirk (professor of criminalistics at the
University of California, Berkeley, and one of the most respected
forensic scientists in the world) to do a complete analysis of the
forensic material in the case.

Kirk examined the prosecution's exhibits: the pillowcase with
the strange bloodstain, Dr. Sam's trousers, and the wristwatch
Dr. Sam had been wearing, which had a bloodstain on it. Why
the watch had been an exhibit is not clear; Dr. Sam had testified that he had felt for Marilyn's pulse when he found her
upstairs, so it was no surprise that the watch was bloodstained.

By the time Kirk was allowed to look at the evidence, the crime was eight months old. But he was still able to arrive at a closely reasoned and intensely detailed conclusion—one dramatically different from the conclusion reached by the police, the district attorney, and the jury.

Kirk was able to re-create the crime from the blood splatters in the bedroom. The blood spots on two of the walls were caused by the direct battering of Marilyn's head, and those on a third wall were from swinging the weapon. Kirk found that a heavy flashlight would have produced wounds like those inflicted on Marilyn, and that there was no sign that anything like a "surgical instrument" had been used. The strange design on the pillowcase, which had so attracted the coroner, was just the result of the pillowcase having been folded over while it was damp with blood.

An area on one side of the bed that was bare of blood showed where the killer must have stood, and its very bareness testified to the tremendous amount of blood that must have fallen on the killer. There was no shower of blood found on Dr. Sam or his clothing that would nearly correspond to what the killer must have received. Kirk was also able to determine that the murder weapon had been held in the assailant's left hand, which was at least indicative. Dr. Sam was right-handed.

Kirk also concluded that, in defending herself, Marilyn must have severely bitten her assailant; there were no bite marks on Dr. Sam. All the bloodstains in the room tested as type O, which was the type of both Marilyn and Sam, but there was one large spot on the door that had an entirely different rate of agglutination than that of the blood of either of the Sheppards. "These differences," Kirk reported, "are considered to constitute confirmatory evidence that the blood on the large spot had a different origin from most of the blood in the bedroom." Unfortunately the bloodstains were now so old that Kirk could investigate no further in that direction.

Despite Kirk's evidence, the Ohio courts were wary of granting the defense's request for a new trial based on new evidence. After all, this evidence could have been developed at the first trial. The fact that the defense had been locked out of the murder house and thus had no access to the bloodstained bedroom was apparently irrelevant. Dr. Samuel Sheppard spent nine years in prison before finally being granted a new trial. The basis of this appeal was that, given the climate of anger in the Cleveland area after the murder, it had been impossible for Sheppard to get a fair trial. In 1966 Dr. Samuel Sheppard was retried and found innocent of the murder of his wife. The guilty party was never caught.

The appearance of a drop of blood that has landed on a surface will vary according to the height from which it was dropped and the surface upon which it lands. On comparatively smooth, flat horizontal surfaces, the drops will be round if the fall is short. Jagged edges will begin to appear as the height is increased, and the jaggedness will increase with the height. If the height is higher than six feet or so, the drops will break up into many smaller drops.

If the object emitting the blood is in motion, the blood drops will be oval and have little tails, which will project in the horizontal direction that the drop was moving. Falling liquids have a characteristic tear-drop shape, tapering toward the top. Since the top lands last, the taper is forward of the main part of the drop. Blood splattered on a wall from a swinging object has a characteristic pattern and shape, which can indicate whether the murder weapon was held in the killer's right or left hand.

Since the size and shape of bloodstains can provide valuable information, an accurate, detailed record of the appearance of such stains must be kept. The technician should photograph all surfaces that show bloodstains, using the best lighting and filter to make them stand out against their background. At the same time it must be recognized that the photographs may be used as evidence, and the manner they are taken can greatly influence both their informational value and their psychological effect on an observer—or on twelve observers in a jury box. A telephoto lens can make them seem more immediate, a wide-angle lens more diffuse; harsh, angular lighting and a green filter will emphasize them, while gentle lighting and a slightly red filter will minimize them. The forensic technician will, of course, resist all such impulses and take the photographs merely as a record of the stains, neither emphasizing nor de-emphasizing their importance photographically. She will also draw a sketch to show the location and shape of the stains, and their relation to the body (if present) and the rest of the crime scene. Distances should be indicated on the sketch.

LARGER BLOOD SPOTS TAKE ON A CHARACTERISTIC
SCALLOPED APPEARANCE.

AS THE HEIGHT FROM WHICH A BLOOD DROP HAS
FALLEN INCREASES, THE SHAPE CHANGES FROM ROUND
TO SCALLOPED TO RAY-EMITTING.

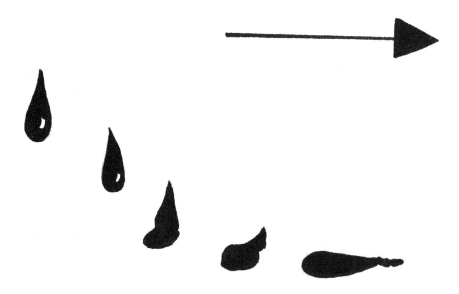

FALLING BLOOD DROPS LEAVE THEIR TAILS IN THE
DIRECTION OF THEIR TRAVEL.

Dr. Paul Kirk, who wrote one of the first books on interpreting bloodstains at a crime scene and who was involved in the reinvestigation of the Marilyn Sheppard murder scene (*see* "The Sam Sheppard Case" *p. 144*), said, "No other type of investigation of blood will yield so much useful information as an analysis of the blood distribution patterns." Blood sprinkles over a wide area may indicate a freely wielded instrument (like an ax) or an active wound being struck hard. An area devoid of blood in an otherwise splattered scene may indicate where the murderer was standing while he committed the crime. The investigator must use caution when interpreting blood-splatter evidence. No single bloodstain can be said to be caused by one particular event. To the eye of an experienced investigator, the pattern in total may paint a picture of the events that caused it, but even then her re-creation of the scene should be framed by caution.

EIGHT

DEOXYRIBONUCLEIC ACID

> *Probably the most exciting, as I view it, of the new techniques emerging for the criminal investigator is the DNA identification technology. Through a genetic pattern-matching process, criminals can now be identified positively by comparing evidence from a crime scene—that is, blood, body fluids, or sometimes a single hair—with that of a suspect.*

— WILLIAM SESSIONS,
DIRECTOR OF THE FEDERAL BUREAU OF INVESTIGATION,
IN A SPEECH BEFORE THE NATIONAL PRESS CLUB ON SEPTEMBER 1, 1988

Back in their forensic laboratory in Gotham City, the criminalists investigating the murder of Godfrey Daniels have finished typing the blood exemplars gathered at the crime scene. Most of the blood is the exact same type as that of the murdered man, but some of it—gathered from the bathroom drain and from spots on the study floor pointed out by the blood-splatter expert—is not. Did Mr. Daniels wound his attacker with the one shot embedded in the wall? Could fate have been so kind as to give the criminalists a sample of the murderer's blood?

Until the past decade a blood sample could point the finger of suspicion at a particular person but was not in itself enough to allow for a certain identification. Blood typing could narrow the possible suspects to approximately 5 percent of the population, but in a city the size of Gotham, with its population of two million, that still left one hundred thousand possible suspects.

But those odds have changed. As the technicians carefully packaged the best of the blood exemplars that were not of the same type as Mr. Daniels's and prepared to send them by overnight mail to CellType Laboratories (an independent lab in a western state that specializes in DNA analysis), they had every hope of being able to match the sample with that of a suspect, if they came across one, and tell with great certainty whether he or she had shed the blood they had found. And putting the suspect at the scene of the crime is a large step in establishing guilt.

In March 1985 twenty-four-year-old Kirk Bloodsworth was convicted by a Maryland court of raping and murdering a nine-year-old girl. He was sentenced to death. Eighteen months later the conviction was reversed for technical reasons, and Mr. Bloodsworth was tried again. He was again convicted, on the testimony of five honest but mistaken witnesses, but this time his sentence was merely life imprisonment.

In June 1993, after spending nine years in prison, Mr. Bloodsworth was released from the Maryland House of Corrections. Shortly thereafter he was given a full pardon by Maryland Governor William Donald Schaefer, and in June 1994 the State of Maryland agreed to pay Mr. Bloodsworth $300,000 as restitution for the years he had spent in prison for a crime they now knew he did not commit. He intends to use part of the money to pay back his father, who "put all his retirement savings, over $100,000, into my defense," and the rest he will use to go to college to earn a degree in mortuary science.

How could the Maryland authorities determine Mr. Bloodsworth's innocence almost a decade after the event and be so positive of their new information that the verdicts of two separate juries were overturned? A new technique called DNA fingerprinting, not available at the time of Mr. Bloodsworth's original trial, enabled forensic serologists to determine that the nine-year-old, dried, desiccated semen stains found on the victim's underwear did not come from Mr. Bloodsworth. If he did not leave the semen, then without question he did not commit the crime. Had DNA tests been available at the time, the state's attorneys affirmed, Bloodsworth would never even have been charged.

On July 15, 1994, Derrick Coleman, star basketball player for the New Jersey Nets, was accused of raping a woman in a Detroit hotel room. Samples of semen taken from the woman during the rape investigation were analyzed; and the DNA information received was compared with that of Coleman. Before the end of July all charges had been dropped when the samples did not match up, thus saving Coleman the stress and expense of a trial and a lot of bad publicity.

On October 21, 1994, Edward Honaker, a forty-four-year-old welder, was released from a Virginia prison after serving ten years. In 1984 he had been convicted of the multiple rape and sodomization of a nineteen-year-old girl and sentenced to three life terms plus thirty-four years. Honaker's lawyers had argued at the trial that sperm found in the victim's body could not be the suspect's because he had had a vasectomy. But both the girl and her boyfriend identified Honaker as the man who had kidnapped her at gunpoint, driven her to a remote mountain cabin, and repeatedly raped her. The prosecution argued that the sperm was from the boyfriend, with whom the girl had had consensual sex before the rape. The jury agreed.

But DNA tests performed on the 10-year-old sample showed that the sperm had not come from the boyfriend and it could not have come from Honaker. Virginia Governor George Allen reviewed the case, double-checked the genetic tests, and ordered Honaker released.

DNA fingerprinting, a technique invented in the mid 1980s by British geneticist Alec Jeffreys, has been responsible for clearing more than two thousand suspects since it became available in 1988, most of them before they were tried and convicted. The technique is based on an analysis of the individual's deoxyribonucleic acid (DNA), which is found in every cell and the structure of which varies from person to person enough to give each one an individual DNA signature.

The two things that make each human being unique are our environment and our heredity. We are born with our heredity, that special combination of genes that makes us what we are, in place. Each of us has a slightly different shuffling of the deck of the hundreds of millions of genetic possibilities (except for identical twins, who share the exact same package of genes). From the moment of birth, environment goes to work, making each of our life experiences different and causing even identical twins to grow into distinct personalities.

But the genetic component is permanent and unchangeable, and is detectable at the cellular level. The blueprint that nature uses to create everything, from a human to a mayfly, is a molecule of DNA. The blueprint remains as part of the structure in every living cell and stays recognizable for a time even after the death of the cell. Recently the bones of a dinosaur found in a coal deposit in Ohio have yielded enough organic material to determine a portion of the sequence of DNA in the long-extinct creature.

DNA fingerprinting or DNA profiling (also occasionally called genetic fingerprinting, though this usage is disappearing) is a complex procedure that as of this writing is not accepted as evidence in every court; however, its acceptability is growing as the methods used are perfected and regularized. Because DNA testing techniques are new and difficult to perform, requiring highly trained technicians, dissent still exists over just how reliable the results are. There is no argument that properly performed DNA tests can establish that a certain sample did not come from a certain individual, but some authorities maintain that the six or so specific places in the DNA strands that are examined may be too similar in two individuals within a comparatively small sampling community to positively differentiate them with the techniques in use today. Therefore they feel it is not possible to state positively that a given sample of DNA came from a given individual, as would be the case, for example, with the positive match of a fingerprint. A reasonable conclusion, they say, is this: If the DNA of an exemplar seems to match the DNA of a suspect, such results affirm that within the population being checked, the odds of another person having DNA that is this close a match is—let us say—one in a hundred thousand. Of course if the two samples do not match, as was the case with Mr. Bloodsworth, then it can be stated positively that the exemplar did not originate with the suspect.

ANASTASIA

In 1994 Dr. Peter Gill, a respected British criminalist, did a DNA testing on tissue samples of Anna Anderson Manahan, who died in 1984 at the age of eighty-three. Anderson had for most of her adult life maintained that she was, in fact, the Grand Duchess Anastasia, youngest child of Tsar Nicholas II of Russia who was murdered with most of his family by the Bolsheviks in 1918, a year after they seized power in Russia. Her story gained credibility in 1991, when Gill used DNA testing on some remains found near Ekaterinburg, in eastern Russia, and established that they were the bones of Nicholas, his wife Alexandra, and three of their daughters. The remains of the tsar's fourteen-year-old son, Alexei, and of one daughter, believed to be Anastasia, were not found.

Unfortunately for the lovers of romantic legend, Gill's testing of the tissue samples also showed that Anderson could not have been related to the tsar. She was most probably a Polish woman named Franzisca Schanzkowska, who was last seen in Berlin in 1920, the same year and location as "Anastasia's" first appearance.

Increasingly, the evidence gathered with experience and an ever increasing database seems to indicate that the fears of the inaccuracy of DNA testing are groundless. A DNA profile can differentiate genetic material to a degree of certainty bordering on the absolute. The chance of finding two individuals with the same DNA, within the limits of current testing, is now estimated to be somewhere between 100 million to one and 30 billion to one.

Part of the ongoing debate has revolved around the fact that different alleles (specific stretches of the DNA molecule) might have different frequencies in different human subgroups; therefore testing for an allele that is rare in one subgroup might overlook the fact that it is common in another. In an effort to be scrupulously fair and err on the side of highest probability, a committee of the National Academy of Sciences recommended in 1992 that in courtroom cases a "ceiling principle" be used to calculate the odds of finding a match. Even using the ceiling principle, the DNA profiling in the worst case would still give odds of two people sharing the same pattern at one in 100,000—which, in most cases, is still good enough. Most authorities now agree on the much higher set of figures.

Human DNA molecules carry coded information that, properly acted upon by the life processes, will cause a baby to be born pretty much in the image of its mother and father. DNA is found in the chromosomes; all genetically normal humans have forty-six, half inherited from each parent. The process of genetic replication was first described in 1865 when Gregor Mendel published the results of his experiments with cross-breeding pea plants. But it took nearly another century for anyone to describe the mechanism: The elegant double-helix model of the DNA molecule first described by Francis Crick and James Watson in 1953 opened the door to understanding the process of sexual reproduction and of evolution.

The DNA molecule is made up of four bases or nucleotides, called Adenine (A), Cytosine (C), Guanine (G), and Thymine (T). They join together in long strands; each strand takes the shape of a spiral, and locked alongside it, twist for twist, is a second strand, the pair forming what Crick and Watson described as a "self-complementary double-helix."

The chemistry of each strand allows the four building-block nucleotides to be arranged in any order, but the order of the adjoining strand is strictly controlled by the order of the first strand. An Adenine can only face a Thymine, and a Cytosine can only face a Guanine. For example, if a segment of the first strand is (quite at random, and uncoiled for easier reading):

A

T

T

T

C

C

G

G

A

C

A

G

T

then its adjoining strand segment must be:

A . . . T
T . . . A
T . . . A
T . . . A
C . . . G
C . . . G
G . . . C
G . . . C
A . . . T
C . . . G
A . . . T
G . . . C
T . . . A

The DNA strands contain the chromosomes' coding information that both make the baby of human design and make it slightly different from all other humans. The ultimate sexual act at the biochemical level involves the uncoiling of these twisted strands and the replication by each single strand of its companion strand—according to these strict rules, out of nucleotides supplied to it by the cell. Thus out of one double helix come two, each identical to the first.

Genetic mutations occur when the replication is less than perfect for some reason, and thus there exists a slight variant in the new instruction set. Many of these mutations are harmless, coding for a slightly different hair or skin color or a slightly more or less efficient enzyme in the body. Many lengths of the DNA helix seem to have no use in the reproductive effort at all, and a mutation in these lengths will have no discernable effect. But some are critical, and a change therein will prove deadly to the forming organism. Because there are more than three billion nucleotides in the human chromosomes, the process of unravelling the function of each chain or combination of chains, though ongoing, will take some time.

But it is not necessary to understand the function of a strand of DNA to use it for identification. Indeed, the apparently useless sections show the most variance from sample to sample. This makes good sense when you consider that a change in a vital section will, if good, give an evolutionary advantage to its possessor and thus enter the general population, while if bad will tend to die out along with its possessor.

Although DNA's function is to blueprint reproduction, a complete copy of an individual's DNA is found in every cell, even those that have nothing remotely to do with reproduction. The only exceptions are sperm and ovum cells, which carry only half of the individual's chromosomes; they combine into one complete set when the sperm penetrates the ovum to begin the process of creating a new person.

So each one of the billions of cells that make up a human being (or an elk or an ostrich or a sturgeon) contains a full copy of the DNA instruction set that went into its creation, which is identical to the DNA in each of the other cells yet ever-so-slightly different from the DNA in anyone else's cells.

The process of digging out the DNA from the cells and examining it is complex and delicate and requires a cautious expertise to accomplish it with the accuracy and certitude necessary for the results to be used as evidence in a courtroom. One of the problems that this new science has faced is in developing a standard of training and competence for its practitioners that will enable a judge to recognize an expert from her credentials.

SECURE IN THEIR PERSONS

The criterion that judges used for many years in deciding whether scientific evidence was admissible in court was known as the Frye Test. Formulated by the United States Court of Appeals for the District of Columbia in 1923 in the case of *Frye* v. *The United States*, the debated issue involved the admissibility of a polygraph (lie detector) test as evidence. The court decided that the major consideration was whether the new scientific technique was generally accepted by experts in that field. It said:

> Just when a scientific principle or discovery crosses the line between the experimental and demonstrable stages is difficult to define. Somewhere in this twilight zone the evidential force of the principle must be recognized, and while

courts will go a long way in admitting expert testimony deduced from a well-recognized scientific principle or discovery, the thing from which the deduction is made must be sufficiently established to have gained general acceptance in the particular field in which it belongs.

Since the Frye decision came down, it has been modified and broadened in both directions. The New York Court of Appeals has ruled (in *People* v. *Middleton*, 1981) that the acceptance of the technique by experts need not be unanimous; the test should be "not whether a particular procedure is unanimously endorsed by the scientific community, but whether it is generally accepted as reliable." While the Second Circuit Court of Appeals, weighing the admissibility of sound voice spectrometry or "voiceprint" evidence (in *The United States* v. *Williams*) said that it was not sufficient for the scientific community to be satisfied as to the utility of a test—the court must also be satisfied. It is the job of the court to weigh the test's "probativeness, materiality, and reliability [against] . . . any tendency to mislead, prejudice, or confuse the jury."

In addition to the question of whether a given test is admissible, there is also the legal problem as to whether it is constitutionally obtainable. In doing a DNA analysis it is necessary to have an exemplar from the suspect to conduct the comparison. If the suspect will not voluntarily give of his or her blood or tissue, can the sample be forcibly taken from him? Or would this violate his Fifth Amendment right against self-incrimination, or possibly even the Fourth Amendment right for citizens to be "secure in their persons" and thus safe from unreasonable search and seizure? One possible way around the latter problem is to obtain a search warrant. The seizure of the DNA sample may be permissible by explaining to a judge what you hope to find and prove, and by getting the judge's signature on a warrant. But should the intrusion of a sharp pointed object—no matter how small—into the suspect's body for the purpose of removing a portion of said subject's tissue—no matter how minuscule—not be regarded in any case as an unreasonable search and seizure?

As to the Fifth Amendment problem, the right against self-incrimination is absolute and cannot be waived at a judge's order. The question is, does it apply to the person's DNA?

A body of case law has been building up as these scientific questions have been asked: Is the taking of a hair sample or testing for blood-alcohol level self-incrimination? Or is a blood test for paternity or disease an unreasonable intrusion on personal liberty?

The Supreme Court settled the Fifth Amendment argument in *Schmerber* v. *The State of California,* deciding that, while the taking of blood is intrusive enough to constitute a search, it did not violate the suspect's Fifth Amendment rights. Self-incrimination is a "testimonial" act, and the compelled production of biological material such as blood or other body fluids does not come under the ban. But the feeling is not unanimous. In a 1957 decision (*Breithaupt* v. *Abrams*), where the Supreme Court found Constitutional approval to taking blood from an unconscious motorist to test his blood-alcohol level, Chief Justice Warren wrote a powerful dissent (joined by Justices Black and Douglas) saying, "law-enforcement officers in their efforts to obtain evidence from persons suspected of a crime must stop short of bruising the body, breaking skin, puncturing tissue, or extracting body fluids, whether they contemplate doing it by force or by stealth."

But the majority of the court, in their opinion, found that taking blood was no longer an unusual event:

> The blood-test procedure has become routine in our everyday life. It is a ritual for those going into the military service as well as those applying for marriage licenses. Many colleges require such tests before permitting entrance, and literally millions of us have voluntarily gone through the same, though a longer, routine in becoming blood donors. Likewise, we note that a majority of our States have either enacted statutes in some form authorizing tests of this nature or permit findings so obtained to be admitted

> in evidence. We therefore conclude that a blood test taken
> by a skilled technician is not such "conduct that shocks
> the conscience" . . . nor such a method of obtaining evi-
> dence that it offends a "sense of justice."

There are several different methods of performing DNA analysis, all of which look for different things within the DNA sample and find those things in different ways. Two of the more recognized are restriction fragment length polymorphism (RFLP) and polymerase chain reaction (PCR), which itself is subdivided into several techniques. Within the next few years the methods of taking DNA samples and testing them should be standardized and simplified, and the use in courtrooms of evidence obtained by DNA profiling will become just as common as the use of fingerprint evidence.

As of this writing the courts of forty-eight states allow DNA evidence, and the other two will probably come around shortly. In November 1994, the appeals court of California upheld the conviction of Frank Lee Soto for the rape of a seventy-nine-year-old woman who subsequently had a stroke and was unable to testify against him. The court ruled that the DNA evidence alone was sufficient to convict. "Because DNA is so highly reliable and relevant, to allow a minor academic debate . . . to snowball to the point that it threatens to undermine the use of it in court is throwing the baby out with the bath water," ruled David G. Sills, the presiding judge.

Perhaps more important than its use in proving the guilt of a suspect is its ability to establish the suspect's innocence. Going through life with the suspicion that you might have committed a horrible crime but had just been lucky enough not to be convicted is psychologically a heavy burden. Being falsely convicted is a terrible burden not only to the person who ends up incarcerated or executed for a crime he did not commit, but also for the state and its citizens, should the error ever become known. And there is also the fact that for every innocent person wrongly convicted, there is a guilty person free to continue committing crimes.

The number of cases in which the DNA evidence has proved crucial is much higher than the number of trials in which such evidence has been offered. Now that it has become clear that DNA testing will be admitted into evidence by the court, many cases where such evidence would have been offered have been closed by plea bargaining instead of going to trial.

NINE

THE SLIGHTEST TRACE

> *They were the footprints of a gigantic hound!*
>
> —————— ARTHUR CONAN DOYLE,
> *THE HOUND OF THE BASKERVILLES*

Working with the aid of powerful searchlights, the Gotham City criminalists carefully searched the area outside the Godfrey Daniels home, both front and back, for six hours after they arrived at the crime scene. In the service area behind the house their search was rewarded: A set of badly defined footprints traveled two houses down to where a car had been parked. There, in the scarcely dried mud from the last rain, were the clear footprints of the car's occupant, along with splendid tire tracks from the car that had been parked there. Working with dental stone, the technicians carefully made casts of the best exemplars from among the footprints and tire tracks. They also drew a map of the back area, showing the location of the track of footprints and the trace of the tires. The searchers also located and carefully bagged a cigarette butt that might have been tossed from the car.

It is not impossible to commit an act of violence without leaving any sign of the act or the perpetrator behind, but it is becoming increasingly difficult. The criminal who leaves neither blood smears nor fingerprints at the scene of the crime may nonetheless have abandoned traces of himself that will unerringly identify him to the patient forensic scientist and her increasingly sophisticated equipment.

A few hairs, a patch of soil, a flake of ash, a scrap of fabric, a mat of fibers, a glass shard, the print of a shoe (or a bare foot), the scratches left by a screwdriver or chisel: Each of these have held sufficient information to end the criminous careers of a variety of industriously light-fingered brethren.

These various exemplars of evidentiary minutia can be looked for in many places: on or about the crime scene, on the person or clothing of the victim or the suspect, in a vehicle that may be connected with the crime, on any object that is suspected of having been removed from the crime scene or is in the possession of either the suspect or the victim.

TOOLS AND THE LAW

As with other innovations in forensic science, the fact that the marks left by one tool could be differentiated from those left by another was not accepted uncritically by the courts. It was not until 1930 that the Supreme Court of the State of Washington cleared the way for such evidence to be routinely used in evidence. Their decision in the case of *Washington* v. *Clark* said, in part:

> Courts are no longer skeptical that by the aid of scientific appliances, the identity of a person may be established by fingerprints. There is no difference in principle in the utilization of the photomicrograph to determine that the tool that made an impression is the same instrument that made another impression. The edge of one blade differs as greatly as the lines of one human hand differ from the lines of another. This is a progressive age. The scientific means afforded should be used to apprehend the criminal.

FOOTPRINTS AND TIRE TRACKS

A criminal who is scrupulous about not leaving any of his fingerprints at the crime scene might carelessly leave a track of well-defined footprints in his wake. While fingerprints have impressed themselves on the common mind, both criminal and pure, as a source of identification, footprints smack of Dr. Thorndyke or Sherlock Holmes and are rarely taken seriously. Unfortunately, in many areas which lack qualified crime labs, they are not taken seriously by the police either.

The print of the bottom of a shoe is distinctive as to class and, with any luck, individual markings. Both the heel and sole of shoes these days tend to have distinctive ridge markings put on by the manufacturer to enhance the running, jumping, or anti-skid properties, or whatever the manufacturer feels will make the shoe more saleable. At any rate they certainly make the print of the shoe more identifiable. And if the shoe has been worn for any length of time, the abrasion wear-marks have quite possibly made the print of that particular shoe different from that of all other shoes.

Prints are left outside in dust, dirt, mud, clay, loam, and snow. They are normally not left inside unless the donor has tracked something into the house, or unless something that will hold a print—like earth, paint, or blood—has been spilled. Often by the time the forensic investigator is on the scene, it has been well walked-over by policemen, detectives, witnesses, and onlookers, obscuring the order and meaning of whatever footprints may be found. If this is so, the logic of the crime scene can be used to determine which footprints might be relevant to the crime. A footprint that is overlaid by another footprint or other marking was made earlier than the overlay. By examining each path of footprints the investigator can determine which was the earliest set; by following them, she can then possibly find one or more footprints that have not been disturbed.

Because a criminal often feels the need to skulk, either in approaching a crime scene or leaving it, a search of the area some distance from the scene and off the more direct approach might be fruitful, especially in suburban or rural settings. It could be that the criminal lurked by a hedge or behind a tree while waiting for the householders to go to bed or to leave the house, or that he approached the crime scene by some back way, not wanting to be seen by passers-by on the road. These areas also offer a greater chance of finding footprints that have not been trampled by onlookers or minions of the law. If the criminal was indeed lurking, the criminalist might even find cigarette butts or other physical evidence left by the suspect. In urban crimes it is a good idea to check the roofs of apartment buildings, when accessible, to see if the criminal was lurking up there.

Tire tracks are even more distinctive. The tire manufacturers have individual tread designs for each separate line of tires sold. The FBI keeps a record of all such tread designs, as do many of the larger forensic labs.

The standard means of preserving footprints or tire prints found in soil or other plastic material is with a mold of dental stone, a casting material made of specially treated gypsum (hydrated calcium sulfate) used by dentists. (Plaster of paris, another form of gypsum, was used in the past, but dental stone is superior.) Cheesecloth or some similar wide-weave material is sometimes laid into the mold for support. The footprint should be boxed off with a frame at least two inches high, and the dental stone batter poured in gently, and not directly onto the print. Dental stone can be used to take impression from packed snow, in which case the footprint should be sprayed first with a fixative such as Snow Print Wax (an item found only in specialized law-enforcement company catalogues). Since dental stone heats up when it is first mixed, some snow or ice should be added to the mix to keep the temperature down if it is being used to take a cast on snow. Unfortunately, when the snow has a crust of ice on top, it is impossible to take a usable cast, or even get reliable information, as the shards of ice in the crust break up any patterns of the shoe print and make measurements of the size of the shoe unreliable.

A careful examination of the casts of footprints can be used not only for identification but also to tell about the movement of the person who made the print. For example, the cast of a walking individual will have an arched appearance; that is, the heel and toe are lower than the middle. This is because a person walking puts more pressure on the ground when his foot hits it, and again when it pushes off for the next step, and thus it sinks in further at the front and rear. The print of a running foot will sink deeper in front, as a runner tends to put less weight on his heel when he lands.

In addition to the footprint itself being a source of potential information, the location and pattern of the footprints are useful. Was the source walking or running? Was he carrying a heavy object? Was he injured? All this can be told from the footprint record of the way he moved across the ground.

CLASS MARKS AND WEAR MARKS FROM THE HEELS OF
SHOES.

All footprints and tire prints should be photographed with a ruler placed alongside for scale. In the case of footprints in soft snow, blood, or other substances where it is impossible or inadvisable to take a cast, the photograph may be the only record. Of course, prints on dirty or dusty surfaces in a house can be "lifted" just as fingerprints are lifted, if a sufficiently wide roll of lifting tape is in the evidence kit.

Although they are not often found, the prints of naked feet are particularly useful evidence, as footprints are as individual as fingerprints. Many hospitals keep prints of newborn babies' feet as part of the birth records, and such prints can be checked against each other for identifying suspects.

TOOL MARKS

The impressions left by the tools used by a burglar to break into a house, a safe, or a bureau drawer can often be used to identify the specific tool. And if the miscreant was unwise enough not to throw the tool away, that bit of false economy could land him in prison. Under a medium-power microscope the sharpest, smoothest-seeming edge will resolve into a jagged line of random serrations. In use the tool picks up wear lines or chips that further distinguish it from all other tools. If the tool is cut, hacked, or chiseled into soft metal or another material that can hold this pattern, a comparison microscope can be used to identify the tool, adding one more link to the chain of evidence against its user.

To identify tool marks, the criminalist will try to remove either the entire marked object or that part of it which has the impression. Since the identifying marks are often minute, a cast is liable to lose detail that would be helpful in the identification.

TOOTHPRINTS

Criminals who leave behind things that they have bitten into, such as apples, bread, or their victim's body, have left behind one more handle by which the criminalist may identify them. If the impression left by the tooth marks can be captured, it can be compared with an impression taken by a dentist of the suspect's teeth.

HAIR

Hair can be typed by species—dog hair is quite different from goat hair is quite different from human hair—and human hair can be typed, to a certain extent, by race. People descended from African ancestors tend to have hair that is flat in cross-section, which is why it is curly. Those with Asian ancestors tend to have hair that is round in cross-section, which is why it is straight. European ancestors have left their descendants with oval hair, which can be straight or curly depending on how oval the cross-section is and how it has been treated. Blond hair is thinner in cross-section than dark hair, and bleaches and dyes on hair can be detected quite easily under the microscope.

Also, by looking at the root of the hair one can tell whether the strand in question was pulled out, cut off, or fell out naturally.

Hair also contains a record of what has been put into the body. As it grows out it contains traces of the nutrients and minerals the body was absorbing at that time. By analyzing Napoleon Bonaparte's hair a century and a half after he died, scientists were able to tell that he had been systematically poisoned with arsenic, although they couldn't be sure that that's what he died of.

Hair contains small amounts of DNA. Thus, if the hair is fresh enough and there is enough of it, it is now possible to determine from just whose head it was removed.

FIBERS

Pieces of wide cellophane tape and vacuum cleaners with special filters are used to gather fiber evidence. Some criminalists prefer one, some the other, based upon their own personal experience. The majority opinion seems to be that forming a cylinder of the tape with the sticky side out, inserting a hand into the cylinder, and rolling it over the suspected area gives the best results. The seats, floor, and trunk of a car are searched for fibers in cases of suspected abduction or the transportation of a murder victim. In the case of Godfrey Daniels, the fiber particles found on the tip of the bullet could be matched to the jacket of the assailant if the jacket is found.

The "Hillside Strangler" case in Los Angeles, where ten young women were raped and strangled and their nude bodies dumped on various hillsides around the city, was solved on the basis of such evidence. Fibers from a victim's clothing were found in the home of the two suspects, Angelo Buono and Kenneth Bianchi, almost two years after the murders. Luckily for the prosecution two of the fiber types were rare and manufactured for only a short time. The evidence was compelling enough to convince a jury, and the suspects were convicted and sentenced to life in prison without the possibility of parole.

TEN

ALL THINGS GREAT
AND SMALL

> By the pricking of my thumbs,
> Something wicked this way comes.

—WILLIAM SHAKESPEARE,
MACBETH

The Gotham City criminalists have now put together their file on the Godfrey Daniels murder case. The DNA evidence isn't back from CellType Labs yet and probably won't be for another couple of weeks. But it won't be needed to catch the killer, only to establish his guilt beyond question—"beyond a reasonable doubt"—at the trial.

A careful comparison of the two unidentified fingerprints recovered from the crime scene has matched them to the fingerprint card of one of Daniels's clients, Philomar "The Yegg" Yancy, a felon with a rap sheet dating back to his youth.

Yancy was picked up for questioning, and he indignantly denied everything. But a forensic team took a cast of the tires on his car, and they matched the tracks found behind Daniels's house. That, along with the fingerprints, gave the police enough probable cause to get a search warrant. A search of Yancy's apartment turned up a pair of shoes matching those that left the shoe prints found near the tire tracks. The investigators also found some very impressive jewelry that did not belong to Mr. Yancy, along with more than eight thousand dollars in bills;

an examination of the bills revealed Godfrey Daniels's fingerprints. Fragments of a torn-up jacket—picked up with sticky tape from the rug—matched the fibers found on the bullet taken from the Daniels's study wall.

Yancy's new lawyer advised him to say nothing, but no words were necessary. A judge gave permission for the investigators to take a blood sample from the suspect, and it was sent for DNA typing.

As an unexpected but welcome bonus, a dishwasher at the Penguin Club found a .32-caliber Walther automatic in the Dumpster behind the restaurant and turned it over to the police. The outside had been wiped clean, but Yancy's fingerprints were found on the clip and on several of the shells. A test firing of the gun showed that it was indeed the murder weapon.

When the DNA tests finally came back, the exemplars from the dead man's study matched Yancy's sample. The trial was short. Yancy was found guilty of murder in the second degree and, as a third-time offender, will probably spend the rest of his life on the grounds of the state prison.

The advances in criminalistics continue, and today's miracle will become tomorrow's commonplace in crime scene investigation. Several states are already establishing DNA databanks for repeat sex offenders, and other criminal classes will certainly be added. Direct real-time fingerprint scanning by computer exists now and will certainly become common, perhaps even as a means of check and credit card verification. Eye retinal scanning techniques have been developed to defeat counterfeiting, in that they can determine a photograph from a living eye. If these methods become ubiquitous, it will be difficult for a felon or an ex-felon to escape notice wherever he or she goes.

Of course, these new adaptations of science to crime-fighting present problems in the fields of personal freedom and social justice. If a person cannot escape the stigma of having once committed a crime, then we are going to have to become wiser as to which crimes deserve the eternal scarlet letter and which allow for genuine rehabilitation.

The one thing we can be sure of is that a book on this same subject written a decade from now will contain chapters describing techniques that we have not yet dreamed of. Unfortunately, this will no doubt be countered by the descriptions of new and more exotic crimes that we do not even have names for today.

Perhaps by then we will have learned that crime prevention by eliminating the root causes is cheaper and more effective than crime punishment—and has fewer victims.

BIBLIOGRAPHY

Ashton-Wolfe, Harry. *The Forgotten Clue*. Cambridge, Mass.: The Riverside Press, 1930.

Berrett, James. *When I Was At Scotland Yard*. London: Sampson, Low, Marston, and Co. Ltd., 1938.

Block, Eugene B. *The Wizard of Berkeley*. New York: Coward-McCann, 1958.

Branham, Vernon C., and Samuel B. Kutash, eds. *Encyclopedia of Criminology*. New York: Philosophical Library, 1949.

Bridges, B. C. *Practical Fingerprinting*. New York: Funk and Wagnalls, 1942 [revised by Charles E. O'Hara, 1963].

Brown, Douglas G., and Alan Brock. *Fingerprints: Fifty Years of Scientific Crime Detection*. New York: E. P. Dutton, 1954.

Fitzgerald, Col. Maurice J. *Handbook of Criminal Investigation*. New York: ARCO, 1974.

Fricke, Charles W., revised by LeRoy M. Kolbrek. *Criminal Investigation (Sixth Edition)*. Store Los Angeles: Legal Book, 1962.

Henderson, Bruce, and Sam Summerlin. *The Super Sleuths*. New York: Macmillan, 1976. [paperback ed.: *The World's Great Detectives and Their Most Famous Cases*. New York: Barnes and Noble, 1981].

Inbau, Fred E. *Lie Detection and Criminal Interrogation* (second edition). Baltimore: The Williams and Wilkins Company, 1948.

Kirk, Paul L., Ph.D. *Crime Investigation: Physical Evidence and the Police Laboratory.* New York: Interscience, 1953.

Laurie, Peter. *Scotland Yard.* New York: Holt, Rinehart and Winston, 1970.

Marsa, Linda, and Don Ray. "Crime Bytes Back," *Omni,* August 1990.

McCallum, John D. *Crime Doctor.* Washington, D.C.: The Writing Works, 1978.

Mackay, Charles. *Extraordinary Popular Delusions and the Madness of Crowds.* London: Office of the National Illustrated Library, 1852.

Morland, Nigel. *An Outline of Scientific Criminology* (Second Completely Revised Edition). New York: St. Martin's Press, 1971.

Neil, Arthur Fowler. *Man-Hunters of Scotland Yard.* Garden City, N.Y.: Sun Dial Press, 1938.

O'Hara, Charles E. *Fundamentals of Criminal Investigation* (Third Edition). Springfield, Mass.: Charles C. Thomas, 1973.

Reid, Sue Titus. *Crime and Criminology* (Second Edition). New York: Holt, Rinehart and Winston, 1979.

Simpson, Keith. *Police: The Investigation of Violence.* Estover, Plymouth, Great Britain: Macdonald and Evans, 1978.

Smith, Bruce, revised by Bruce Smith Jr. *Police Systems in the United States* (Second Revised Edition). New York: Harper and Row, 1960.

Smith, Sir Sydney. *Mostly Murder.* New York: David McKay Company, 1959.

Söderman, Harry. *Policeman's Lot.* New York: Funk and Wagnalls, 1956.

——— and John J. O'Connell. *Modern Criminal Investigation.* New York: Funk and Wagnalls, 1935 (First Edition), 1952 (Fourth Edition).

Stead, Philip John, ed. *Pioneers in Policing.* Montclair, N.J.: Patterson Smith, 1977.

Sullivan, John L. *Introduction to Police Science.* New York: McGraw-Hill, 1966.

Thomson, Sir Basil. *The Story of Scotland Yard.* New York: The Literary Guild, 1936.

Thorwald, Jurgen. *Crime and Science: The New Frontier in Criminology.* New York: Harcourt, Brace, and World, 1967.

Vollmer, August. "The Prevention and Detection of Crime as Viewed by a Police Officer," *Modern Crime,* May 1926.

Walls, H. J. *Scotland Yard Scientist: My Thirty Years in Forensic Science.* New York: Taplinger, 1973.

Wensley, Frederick Porter. *Forty Years of Scotland Yard.* New York: Garden City Publishing, 1930.

INDEX

D

T